SOWABLE WORD

HELPING ORDINARY PEOPLE LEARN TO LEAD BIBLE STUDIES

Peter Krol

For Mark Fodale,
who first sold me on
the delightful glory of
interactive small-group Bible study

CruciformPress

"**If you are looking for a simple, practical way to lead group Bible studies more effectively, this is it.** Oftentimes, books on Bible study will either focus on the Bible part or group dynamics. In *Sowable Word*, Peter combines both. Get this book and use it yourself or give it to your small group leaders in your ministry or church. They will be glad you did."

> **Dr. Tim Lane**, President, Institute for Pastoral Care, and Tim Lane & Associates; author of *Unstuck: A Nine-Step Journey to Change that Lasts*

"*Sowable Word* is Peter Krol's great sequel to his *Knowable Word*. Whether you are new to leading a Bible study or an old hand at it, this book will equip you with tools and encourage you with zeal to lead a group into the Word. *Sowable Word* is **well-organized, biblical, thoughtful, seasoned, humble, practical, doable, readable and fresh**—what more can you want from a book?"

> **Tedd Tripp**, pastor, author, and speaker

"Learning to live well in Christian community is the task of every believer. And for that, preparing men and women to assist others in the study of the Bible is essential. **I know Peter Krol, and through him, some of the dozens of Bible teachers and small group leaders he has trained over the years. We owe him our thanks for *Sowable Word*.** For in it, the confidence many need to begin leading others in the joyful study of God's Word can be acquired."

> **David Helm**, Senior Pastor, Christ Church Chicago; Chairman, The Charles Simeon Trust

"*Sowable Word* is **a simple but powerful resource** to give us practical help in studying the Word, then preparing and leading bible studies. **Any believer** who desires to dig deep and share biblical truths with others **will benefit greatly** from the guidance and skills Peter Krol gives us."

> **Steve Shadrach**, Center for Mission Mobilization

"Whether you think you could never lead a Bible study group, or may be struggling with the whole task, or perhaps have been doing it for years but have grown a bit weary, this book is for you. Based on his 20 years of experience, Peter Krol has produced a positive, attractive, and very readable guide to the whole process of studying Scripture effectively in a group setting. **Following through with these insights is like having a personal coach work alongside you** to help you develop and hone your skills, both in handling the text and relating to the group members. Best of all, the book is **thoroughly Biblical**, in the principles it identifies and the practice it illustrates. This is **an excellent training manual for a task of lasting importance** to groups of Christian believers around the world. I warmly recommend it."

> **David Jackman,** Past President, the Proclamation Trust, London, UK.

"If you want to learn how to lead and write your own Bible studies, this book will help you do it. Peter Krol gives an accessible, practical guide for how to create a Bible study that people actually want to attend. **The tools he puts forward are simple and effective. A novice leader will learn, and an experienced leader will be refined."**

> **Colleen McFadden,** Women's Ministry Director, Trinity Community Church; Director of Women's Workshops, Charles Simeon Trust

"So often I hear people referencing a Bible study of which they are a member reading through a book written about the Bible, not the Bible itself. I believe this is because many leaders today feel intimidated by teaching directly from God's Word for a myriad of reasons. This is exactly why *Sowable Word* was written and is desperately needed. In it, Peter Krol gives **biblical, practical, step-by-step wisdom to every level of Bible study leader**. There is not one element of Bible study leadership that is left unconsidered in this thoughtful, easy-to-use guide. It **should be on the shelf of every serious leader."**

> **Vince Burens,** CEO/President, The Coalition for Christian Outreach

"Peter Krol is persistent. He wants you and your friends to study the Bible together the most effective way. **His website,** *Knowable Word,* **is a favorite of mine** and I have recommended it and passed along his articles many times. Now, he has gathered up some of his wisdom and persistence about teaching Bible studies into a book to help us do just that, and do it well. *Sowable Word?* — by all means. Read it and do it."

> **Jim Elliff,** Founder and President, Christian Communicators Worldwide

Don't miss this companion volume from Peter Krol

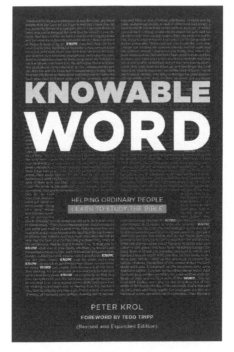

Knowable Word: Helping Ordinary People
Learn to **Study the Bible**

(Revised and Expanded Edition)

Sowable Word: Helping Ordinary People Learn to Teach Bible Studies

Print / PDF ISBN: 978-1-949253-30-6
ePub ISBN: 978-1-949253-32-0
Mobipocket ISBN: 978-1-949253-31-3

Contents

Part 1

Building a Foundation

When God's Word falls on good soil, he promises the results will astound (Mark 4:8). That's why there's a surprising glory in leading a group of ordinary people to open their Bibles, read what's on the page, and discuss how God might use those words to change the world.

Perhaps you fear "getting it wrong" without expert guidance from a workbook or study guide. Is it possible to lead fruitful and engaging groups that actually study *the Bible*?

You might be familiar with the OIA method of Bible study (*Observe, Interpret, Apply*), but is it safe for you to *lead others* in OIA Bible study? (If you are not familiar with this method, have no fear. Chapter 2 will bring you up to speed.)

I wrote this book to encourage you in this task. I will present the unique opportunities and objectives of Bible studies. I will suggest ways to lead Bible studies that speak to both believers and non-believers. I will explain how to start a group, how to prepare for meetings, and how to lead a discussion. I will warn you of potential pitfalls, and I will cast a vision for training others to lead after you. Whether you are a new Bible study leader or a pastor who's been doing it for years, I trust these ideas can help you to hone your craft.

The first part of this book will build foundations for Bible studies that actually study the Bible. I'll provide definitions and goals, such as what Bible studies are and why we have them. Then I'll summarize the Direct-OIA Bible study method, which equips us to lead others in Bible study. Finally, I'll address the basic skills required to get a group started.

I commend you for embracing this mission to lead others in study of God's Word. Through that Word, you might introduce some to the Lord Jesus Christ for the first time. And through that same Word, you can shepherd others unto maturity of faith. Your ministry may have seasons of planting and seasons of watering, but God alone is able to save souls and cause growth (1 Corinthians 3:6). He does such work through the implanted Word (James 1:21).

Therefore, there is something indescribably wonderful that happens when people learn to engage with God directly through his Word. People who are used to merely being told what to do learn to hear God's own voice. People afraid of messing up gain the confidence to take up and read. Consumers of content develop into distributors of truth. Committed disciples grow into influential disciple-makers.

And you now get to be a part of it. Let's see how.

One

Why Lead Bible Studies?

Have you ever had a conversation like this?

"What do you have going on tonight?"

"I'm going to Bible study."

"Great! What part of the Bible are you studying?"

"Francis Chan's *Crazy Love.*"

What Is a Bible Study?

Now, I'm no Chan-hater. I've never read *Crazy Love*, and probably I should have. But let's be honest: while discussing a book can be a great use of your time, it's fundamentally different than studying the Bible. It's really a book club or a reading group.

A group Bible study is… wait for it… *a group of people studying the Bible.* So when I say, "Bible study," I don't mean a reading group, a prayer meeting, a hymn sing, a revival service, a sermon, or a classroom lecture. And for purposes of this book I don't mean individual study. I'm referring to a group of people (which could be small or large) actively engaged in examining Scripture together.

Your commitment to leading Bible studies that

actually study the Bible will typically require you to take your group through selected books of Scripture. Therefore, though you may want to kick off each new series with an overview of the book under consideration, most of your subsequent meetings will involve an OIA discussion of a portion of the text.

Many Bible studies, of course, use a pre-packaged study guide or curriculum, and when these reflect a close adherence to the OIA method they can be valuable. But this book reflects my position—that the best studies will be unfiltered. Why? Because (as we will cover in more detail later in this book), although the main point of a given passage of Scripture never changes, how we think about it, talk about it, and apply it to our lives can vary in countless ways.

Indeed, this is why the Bible is uniquely valuable across history and across cultures, as it brings eternal, unchanging truth to bear on individual lives and societies. And it is why I'm interested in training people to study the Bible itself, directly. Of course, we shouldn't *ignore* what others have said about the Bible. We're a part of the community of faith, and we should never imagine that we can study the Bible in a vacuum and have a corner on the truth. But at the same time we must always evaluate what others say in light of what the text of Scripture says. Because if we never learn how to find what the text says, we're no different from the blind leading the blind. And that never ends well (Luke 6:39).

And what if your group or church leadership prefers that you use a curriculum? Then what you learn in this book will supercharge your use of it. If the curriculum is truly OIA in nature, you'll see its strengths and be able to maximize them. If it falls short, you'll be able to bring in any missing elements and put less emphasis on any content or techniques that distract from a close focus on the words of the passage itself.

In fact, to drill down a little further, what I'm doing in this book is to teach you how to help others discover *God's intended message* in any passage of Scripture. When you are able to do that, your group will obtain the greatest possible benefit from additional resources, because you will have a divine measuring rod against which to evaluate what those resources teach.

I propose that commentaries and study guides are most beneficial to us when we treat them as *conversation partners.* We consider what they have to say, but only insofar as they direct our attention back to the text. To ignore them altogether is hubris. To use the wrong ones makes us morally culpable for any resulting damage to people's souls. To use even good ones as our *source of authority* could make us slaves to every wind of doctrine—or it could inadvertently communicate to our group members that ordinary people simply can't be trusted with sacred things.

Therefore, regardless of which resources enter the conversation and how they do so, the living and abiding Word of God ought to be the main course we serve our people.

Why Have Bible Studies?

If Bible studies, rightly understood, are groups of people actively engaged in examining Scripture together, then they differ from sermons, classroom lectures, and informal instruction in that they consist primarily of group discussion. And this means, especially for leaders, that Bible studies can be terrifying. You never know what people will say… you might not know what to say in response… what if you lose control of the discussion? I admit, the prospect of leading a group in the way I propose can be daunting.

But while the best discussion is unscripted, it does not have to be out of control. Though open-ended, it doesn't have to be directionless. Though interrogative, it can still be powerfully declarative.

This is because Bible studies have something going for them that few sermons or personal quiet times can achieve: *interaction*. This is the chief advantage of Bible studies, and we see it playing out in all kinds of ways.

Because of interaction, we can see what part of the passage is hitting the mark with our group. This allows us to adjust in the moment to make better use of what's connecting with people's hearts, and jettison whatever is unhelpful.

Because of interaction, we can assess how people

are responding to the text. We get a good idea of what to follow up on later in personal conversations.

Because of interaction, we can see the fruits of faith or unbelief. We can often gauge where people are in their walks with the Lord as we see them wrestling with his Word.

Because of interaction, we can address difficult topics frankly. Some issues, normally considered impolite for pleasant conversation, may find safe harbor in an engaging Bible discussion. For example:

- What are some bad spending habits we should repent of?
- How can you be a more Christ-like father or mother?
- Last week you mentioned how stressed out you were. How does today's passage speak to your stress?
- What does Jesus say about how to receive eternal life? How would that affect your life if it were true?

Because of interaction, we can witness something extraordinary: the softening of human hearts. Sometimes people change their minds or their convictions over the course of a single discussion. At other times, it will take place over weeks, months, or even years. Sometimes we'll notice an improvement in attitude or character before the changed person even becomes aware of it.

Because of interaction, we can multiply our ministries. Through discussions, we can teach people how to study the Bible for themselves. We can train assistant leaders who will eventually lead their own Bible studies. We can coach people in particular skills such as making small talk, asking questions, listening attentively, or sharing vulnerably.

Because of interaction, people often feel respected and appreciated. This feeling encourages greater commitment and risk.

Because of interaction, we can better understand others and help them feel understood. God, who knows all things, chose to *interact* with Adam and not merely declare truth to him: "Where are you?" (Genesis 3:9). Jesus, who knew what was in the heart of a man, chose to *interact* and draw out others' thoughts: "Is this what you are asking yourselves, what I meant?" (John 16:19).

As you learn how to lead better Bible studies, don't fail to make use of your chief advantage: interaction.

Why Do People Join Bible Studies?

So yes, interaction is invaluable, but a fundamental question remains: *Why* should we interact together about the Bible? What is our goal? What are we after? We could do many activities in groups—why study the Bible instead of doing something else?

Except for the rare cynic or mocker, nearly

everyone who joins a Bible study does it for reasons that are good. But good reasons become problematic when they supplant the best reasons. Watch out for the following reasons people might have for starting or joining a Bible study:

1. To learn about the Bible.

2. To support their church or its people in the study.

3. To sit under a gifted leader.

4. To be part of something great.

5. To make new friends or deepen existing friendships.

6. To be in a supportive environment.

7. To build a tightly knit community.

8. To develop more theological insight.

9. To grow as a Christian.

Those reasons are all good. We *should* have Bible studies for such reasons. But good reasons are only good when the best reason—to know God through his Son Jesus Christ (John 17:3, Philippians 3:7–11, Ephesians 1:16–17)—is continually kept front and center. Indeed, all good reasons will be served far better when we focus chiefly on the best reason.

God spoke his Word to show himself to us. And God's Word became flesh and dwelt among us (John

1:14). Though God spoke in many ways to the prophets, he has now spoken his Word in these last days by his Son: the glory of God, the imprint of God's nature, the only purification for sin, and the supreme power in all the universe (Hebrews 1:1–4).

We invite people to Bible studies so we can introduce them to Jesus (Acts 17:2–3). And we lead Bible studies so they may find eternal life by knowing God and his Son Jesus Christ (John 17:3). And whether they don't yet profess faith, or they have been walking with Christ for decades, their greatest needs are still to be "introduced" to Jesus in greater depth, and to revel in the eternal life of knowing him. God has made himself knowable, and we study his knowable Word so we might know Jesus, the living Word.

Winsome community and cogent education are terrific recruiters. But let's make sure we give people something that will address their deepest needs and last for eternity.

Will Your Bible Study Be Group-Centered or Christ-Centered?

So the chief *advantage* of the group format is interaction and the main goal of group Bible studies is to help people know God through his Son Jesus Christ.

But sometimes that chief *advantage* can steal the limelight, and the main *goal* becomes the understudy.

Or if you prefer the athletic over the theatrical: the chief *advantage* can steal the ball, and the main *goal* gets benched. However you frame it, the result is the same: we get so excited by positive interactions between group members that our focus subtly slides from knowing God to knowing each other. And since knowing each other is a great thing, we might not even notice the shift.

Here are some questions to help you evaluate whether your Bible study is group-centered or Christ-centered. You may want to return to these questions periodically to evaluate your group's progress toward the right goal:

- Do group members spend more time sharing about their problems or testifying to God's grace in their lives?

- Does your Bible study always land on the same applications, or is there a sense of forward movement and invigorating variety?

- Do people depend on the leader to do all the thinking, or do they actively engage in the study?

- Is there general agreement and affirmation on most things, or do people feel free to challenge and disagree with one another?

- If the leader were to stop leading the group, would the group have another leader trained and ready to take over, or at least heading in that direction?

- How long has it been since new people joined the group? Is the group so ingrown that new people would have a hard time fitting in?

- If any unbelievers unexpectedly showed up, would they meet God among you (1 Corinthians 14:24–25)?

- If your group discussed a secular self-help book instead of the Bible, would the discussion look any different?

From day one, seek to set strong cultural norms in your group, since these can be difficult to change once they become established (Chapter 3 will guide you in that). But before we can try to lead others, we must know how to study the Bible for ourselves.

•

Two

Summary of the OIA Method

Before we can lead Bible studies that actually study the Bible, we must be able to study the Bible for ourselves. This chapter — which abridges material from my book *Knowable Word: Helping Ordinary People Learn to Study the Bible* (Cruciform Press, 2014, 2022) — serves as a reminder of the OIA process. [1]

A Simple and Reasonable Method

Whether you are a pastor or elder, a small-group leader or Sunday school teacher, a conscientious parent or enthusiastic evangelist, the Lord calls you to rightly handle his Word of truth, without any need for shame (2 Timothy 2:15). Therefore, while we need the research of scholars to preserve and deepen knowledge, our fundamental method for Bible study must not require a graduate education or academic pedigree. Nor must it assume a library of knowledge or a specific set of cultural expectations.

There must be a simple method for Bible study that transcends history, geography, generational divides, and cultural norms. This method must not bore scholars, and it must not leave school children behind. It should take only moments to learn but a lifetime to perfect. It should work for anyone of any age in any place at any time.

You have such a method already, and you use it all the time. You're using it right now. You follow this method every time you communicate with another person, dead or alive, through written or oral means. Perhaps you do it so instinctively you've never thought of it as a method.

1. *Observe*—What does it say?

2. *Interpret*—What does it mean?

3. *Apply*—How should I respond?

That's it. Your toddler niece does it when she *observes* her mother hand her a bottle, *interprets* the gesture as an offer of liquid treasure, and *applies* the event's meaning by seizing the bottle and taking a swig. Someone's great-great-great grandpa did it back in the Old World when he *observed* a customer enter his humble shop, *interpreted* the arrival as potential business, and *applied* the situation by smiling, welcoming the customer, and pitching his wares.

Think about reading the news, hearing a lecture, talking on the phone, communicating non-verbally with someone you just met, attending a business meeting, listening to music, watching TV, debating an issue, texting, or going on a date. Every act of meaningful communication between two individuals—even when done across time through a book—can be broken down into three steps: Observe, Interpret, and Apply.

OIA. It's really that simple.

How OIA Helps Us to Use the Bible Rightly

What would happen if you ignored any of those three steps? Imagine you're a homebuilder, and the buyer has communicated his intentions to you through a series of plans. Fail to *observe* the plans, and you'll end up with an "interesting" house not up to code or customer satisfaction. Fail to *interpret* the plans, and you may end up with a geothermally heated yacht, completely missing the designer's intention. Fail to *apply* the plans, and you won't stay in business for long; nobody wants to pay you to go golfing.

Picture how challenging it can be to communicate with someone who lacks one or more of the three skills required for those steps. When someone can't or won't observe the facts, we look for evidence of disability. Those unable to interpret the main idea communicated to them, we may see as aloof or socially awkward. And if they consistently fail to apply the main idea, we might call them lazy or irresponsible. In each case, we must adjust our expectations and fill in the gaps before communication can take place.

God has communicated to us through his Word,

the Bible. And communication hits its mark through OIA. So to understand what God has spoken, we must use the OIA method when studying the Bible. What matters most is not the exact terminology of OIA, but the substance of it. Many people say the same thing with different terminology: inductive Bible study, COMA, SOAR, CIA, the Swedish Method, and the grammatical-historical method of biblical interpretation are all essentially OIA with different names. So when I say, "we must use the OIA method on the Bible," please don't misread me to be saying "anyone who doesn't use the terms *observe*, *interpret*, and *apply* must be misusing the Bible." I'm merely saying we must read the Bible the same way we normally communicate with other people.

So how can normal people do this in their Bible study?

Observe

Great Bible study begins with a few basic mechanics. Whether you're an untested rookie or a seasoned professional, you can always improve at observing the following five elements of literature. Before you can interpret what the Bible means, you must develop mastery in observing what it says.

> **1. Literary Form.** What kind of writing is it? Is this passage primarily narrative, discourse, or poetry? Does it have any secondary forms

embedded within the main form (for example, a speech-discourse embedded within a larger narrative; or narrative statements scattered throughout a lengthy poem)?

2. **Words**. Count how many times key words are repeated. Notice how various things are described or labeled. Keep track of how the narrator names the characters through the passage, and whether he changes their names or titles along the way.

3. **Grammar**. Identify the subject, verb, and object of each sentence. What are the main verbs? (This isn't as scary as it sounds; you're just looking for the actors and their actions.) In other words: who does what, and to whom or what is it done?

4. **Structure**. How does the passage fit together? Break it into paragraphs or stanzas. Notice transitions and linking words.

5. **Mood**. What tone does the author use? Does the passage inspire action, evoke emotion, or challenge assumptions?

Too many "biblical" arguments fail to observe the text carefully. For example, just pick up any tract from the Watchtower Society to find Bible-saturated arguments that Jesus is not God, the Holy Spirit is not a person, God's kingdom was established in 1914, holiday celebrations are sacrilegious, and blood transfusions are immoral. Without careful observation, your study will never find an anchor within the text. Therefore, observation is a critical first step.

Interpret

The OIA method can be diagrammed in the shape of an X. The first part of the process (explained in the previous section) is to make as many observations as possible. Next we tackle *interpretation*. This involves investigating our observations through questions and answers until we understand the text's meaning (the author's main point).

Since we'll continue observing new things in God's Word until Jesus returns, our observations could be infinite in number. But interpretations are not infinite (though our grasp of them may mature over time). Biblical authors had agendas, and we are not authorized to alter or add to those agendas. We scrutinize the facts of the text until we're able to think the author's thoughts after him. And since biblical authors wrote God's very words, good interpretation trains us, with the help of the Holy Spirit, to think God's thoughts. It's like when husbands and wives complete each other's sentences, only better.

Three steps will help you conduct a sound and responsible investigation.

Ask questions of your observations. With your

observations as the raw materials of your study, investigate them further by peppering them with questions. What does that term mean? Who are the main characters and what is their history? Why is that word repeated? Why did the author shift from narrative to poetry and back? What do the connector words suggest about the author's chief argument? What are the grounds for that conclusion? Why is the passage structured as it is? How does one section relate to another? So what does the author expect his readers to believe or do as a result of what he's written?

Answer the questions from the text. Once you have asked your questions, answer them. But there's one critical rule: answer questions only if they are answered — explicitly or implicitly — in the text (Proverbs 30:5–6). If the answer is stated explicitly, find it. If you have reason to believe the original audience would have known the answer to your question because it was simply part of their history or culture, make use of a resource to help you cross the cultural divide. But if your questions are not clearly answered or assumed in the text at hand, let them go for now. Other texts will most likely take them up. Your job is to understand the point this author wishes to make in this text.

Determine the author's main point. Your investigation should lead you to the main point of the passage. Sometimes the author's main point is explicit (for example, Hebrews 8:1), but many times it's not.

Either way, uncovering the main point should be the goal of interpretation.

The main points of Bible passages are the ones worth fighting for because they represent the primary things God wants us to understand. We may draw conclusions about secondary or debatable points, but such conclusions must never drown out the Bible's main points in our thinking or teaching (Matthew 23:23–24).

Once you know the author's main point, you're ready to move into the bottom part of the X diagram. First, you must complete the work of interpretation by connecting the text's message to the person and work of Christ (labeled "Gospel" on the diagram). Three questions will help you to see Jesus in the Scripture just as he saw himself there (Luke 24:46–47):

- What does this passage have to say about the Messiah's death and resurrection?

- How does it expose our need to repent of sin and be forgiven?

- In what way does it open to every nation this message of forgiveness through the risen Messiah?

Now you are ready to apply the main point to your situation or audience.

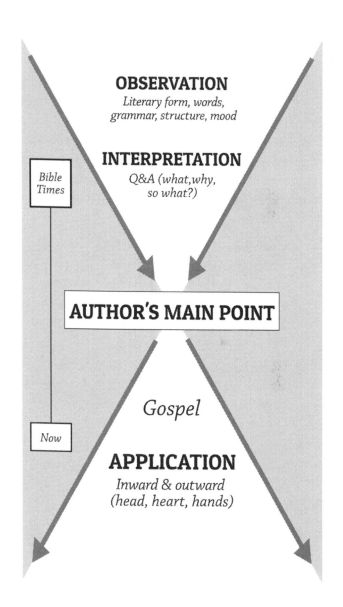

Apply

Explaining why Christians should apply the Bible is almost like explaining why lovers should kiss or why children should open birthday presents. Good things delight the soul, and true delight can't be captured in a numbered list. There's something magical and beautiful in the diligent application of Scripture, so I wish I could simply say, "It's more fun than a prepaid Amazon shopping spree," but this important question warrants at least four concrete answers.

1. **Christians should apply the Bible because we know God.** Though we still have sin, we don't love it like we used to. We have a new allegiance, and the lover of our souls offers a promising alternative to our old habits, values, and patterns of thinking.

2. **Christians should apply the Bible because we are known by God.** He knew us before we ever knew him, and he has vowed to make us more like Jesus.

3. **Christians should apply the Bible because we are free from sin's dominion.** We're not stuck in the old way of doing things. We don't have to keep hurting ourselves and the people we love. We're free to do what God wants us to do, which is always the best thing we could do.

4. **Christians should apply the Bible because...**

APPLICATION WORKSHEET

Text: _____

	Inward	Outward
Head		
Heart		
Hands		

we are Christians! A static life is inconsistent with true faith. According to 1 John, we'll know we have eternal life by three pieces of evidence: confessing Christ, loving others, and keeping God's commandments. These proofs don't imply sinlessness—John expects us to repent often and be forgiven (1 John 1:8–2:2)— but they do mean our lives should change over time to better reflect what God wants for us.

Bible application is the challenging art of producing change. We develop proficiency at such application by considering three spheres: head, heart, and hands. These spheres represent three aspects of human life where we can both change and help others to change. As we will see, Paul suggested these three spheres of application when he taught his protégé Timothy how to use the Bible (2 Timothy 3:14–17).

The head represents everything we think and believe. Head application means being a hearer of the Word. This sphere involves thinking God's thoughts after him and believing what he says. In this sphere, we meditate on the attributes and nature of God the Father, Son, and Holy Spirit. We identify the lies we believe and replace them with the truth. With our heads, we remember the gospel: "But as for you, continue in what you have learned and have firmly believed, knowing from whom you learned it and how from childhood you have been acquainted with the sacred writings, which are able to make you wise for salvation through faith in Christ Jesus" (2 Timothy 3:14–15).

The heart represents who we are on the inside—our desires and allegiances. Heart application is the first and foundational part of being a doer of God's Word. This sphere involves worshiping God above all and considering others more important than ourselves. As the seed of the gospel takes deep root, we set aside our old loves and instead begin to love God and others. The gospel, now internalized, shapes our hearts according to the Lord's own righteousness. "All Scripture is breathed out by God and profitable for teaching, for reproof, for correction, and for training in righteousness" (2 Timothy 3:16).

The hands represent everything we do. Hands application is the second part of being a doer of the Word. This sphere involves laying aside our old patterns of selfish behavior, imitating the Lord and his ambassadors, and becoming more effective at building God's Kingdom. Thus, the gospel begins to bear fruit "that the man of God may be complete, equipped for every good work" (2 Timothy 3:17).

Finally, even in our personal study, we can apply the Bible in two directions: inward and outward. Inward application considers how *I* need to change in the three spheres of head, heart, or hands. Outward application considers how *I can help others* to consider how God may want them to change in the three spheres of head, heart, or hands. Right now, both directions involve ways you can apply the Bible. Later in the book, I'll discuss the mechanics of helping others in a small group setting.

God desires to bring about change in all three spheres—head, heart, and hands—and in both directions—inward and outward—but many people just naturally incline toward only one or two boxes on the worksheet. The trick of application is to address all areas without imbalance.

Effective Teachers Trace Out the Steps

Children learning to communicate don't focus on the process itself. They're not breaking down the components of effective communication in order to ask for some milk. No, these steps become so instinctive they emerge with astonishing ease.

In the same way, seasoned students of the Bible typically put the skills of OIA Bible study into practice without drawing attention to them. The more you practice, the easier it will be to catch the Bible's ideas without getting overwhelmed by all the words on the page. And yet, to teach these skills to others, we must be able to back up and trace out the steps for them. If you would like more guidance in this, you can find it in my book *Knowable Word*, which offers many illustrations of the principles, along with practice exercises for you to consider.

A Concluding Caution

Let me conclude this chapter with a simple caution. As you observe, interpret, and apply, the most important thing is always to do so *in context*. Read each verse in the context of the chapter, each chapter in the context of the section, each section in the context of the book, and each book in the context of the Bible. Context makes all the difference.

For example, Paul's command to "rejoice in the Lord" (Philippians 4:4) takes on a new light when you see it's one step in the reconciliation process between Euodia and Syntyche (Philippians 4:2–9), which itself is a prime example of the joyful unity Paul seeks for the church (the main point of the letter of Philippians).

Observe, interpret, and apply. Do this well, and you'll be able to help others do the same.

Three
Starting a Group

So you've been convinced that ordinary people can, in fact, learn to study the Bible. And you'd like to help others learn these skills for themselves in the context of an interactive small group. To get the group started, you should consider the group's identity, expectations, and recruitment.

Group Identity

Often we distinguish Bible studies by the type of people we're trying to reach. The strength of this approach lies in putting yourself in other people's shoes and designing your Bible study to best serve the group, making you like an expert marksman selecting a firearm based on the distance, size, and shape of the target.

So you might think in the following categories:

- Investigative (or evangelistic) Bible studies introduce *unbelievers* to the claims of Jesus in the Gospels. We might call these groups "Bible discussions" instead of "Bible studies" to make them more palatable to unchurched people.

- Growth Bible studies help *professing believers* to deepen their walks with Christ.

- Brief devotional Bible studies help *committee members* or *retreat participants* to ground their meetings in truth from God's Word.

- Training Bible studies teach people how to study the Bible for themselves and thus equip *mature believers* to use careful OIA skills in their personal Bible study.

- Leadership Bible studies encourage *church or small group leaders* with biblical principles for shepherding others with the Word.

Such categories help us to lay down our lives for others and tailor our approach to their needs. When we think proactively about who will attend, we labor for a positive user experience.

However, this approach has a few dangers.

- We might be led to believe some Bible study groups need to focus on the gospel, while others need to focus on the Christian life or discipline or growth. But we should see the gospel of Jesus Christ in every passage of Scripture, regardless of who attends the study. [a]

- We might expect some Bible studies to focus on application and other studies to focus on education. But God wrote the Scripture to

---

a. See Chapter 3 of my book, *Knowable Word: Helping Ordinary People Learn to Study the Bible* (Cruciform Press, 2014, 2022), the section titled, "How to See Jesus in Any Bible Passage."

produce change in all who read it. No Bible studies should be mere intellectual exercises.

- In focusing on how best to know the people who attend the Bible study, we might slide away from the main goal of Bible study, which is to know God through Jesus Christ.

As you consider what your Bible study's identity will be, defining the group by its commitment level may help you avoid those dangers.

- *Low commitment* Bible studies work best for situations where we need to make it as easy as possible for people to get into the Word. The leader expects people simply to show up and take part in the discussion as they are able. Such studies work well as five-minute introductions to business meetings, as short investigative studies (for people exploring Christianity), or as introductions to the OIA method of Bible study.

- *Moderate commitment* Bible studies work best for situations where people want more out of the Scriptures, but they still need a lot of guidance. In such studies, the leader expects people to commit, at least, to attending the study and reading the passage beforehand. At the meeting itself, the leader might not read the text but can dive right into the discussion.

- *High commitment* Bible studies work best for

situations where people need to be challenged beyond what they might find comfortable. In such studies, the leader expects people to spend one to five hours independently studying the passage before each meeting. The leader may expect group members to arrive ready to share what they think is the author's main point.

The key to elevating people's commitment is to give them homework. Don't assume people can't handle homework or that homework expectations will push them away. If we give them a vision for it, many people will understand that they get out of the study as much as they put into it. And they'll place higher value on things that cost them more. Believers and unbelievers both can be inspired by such expectations.

When we distinguish types of Bible studies by the required degree of commitment, however, one particular danger is that we may have group members asking for differing degrees of commitment. In a single Bible study, we're likely to ask too much of some people and too little of others. At such times, it may be helpful to split the group into different studies with different commitment levels. Or we may need to feed a ready-for-higher-commitment person with an opportunity to co-lead the study or receive more training outside the study.

As I lead Bible studies, I seek to evaluate whether I'm calling attendees to a commitment commensurate with their maturity and Christ's expectations for them (Matthew 11:28–30, Luke 9:57–62). And I make frequent changes based on what is most appropriate at the time.

Expectations

The first Bible study I attended in college was a terrible disappointment to me. I arrived armed with my new *NIV Study Bible*—a graduation present from my gram—and fresh out of Christian summer camp, ready to get busy. At that meeting, however, no one else had a Bible. We never spoke of the Bible. I don't think Jesus came up much either, except as an alternative lifestyle option. After the study, I wept as I walked back to my dorm, fearing I had missed the Rapture, for surely I was the only Christian left on earth.

Expectations are funny things. We all have them, but we usually don't realize what they are until they're not met. Sometimes we set them disappointingly low in an effort to avoid disappointment. Sometimes we set them frustratingly high, thereby self-fulfilling our frustration. We wield our expectations like hot pokers to get people moving in our preferred direction.

Although expectations can be abused, they aren't always a bad thing. God has expectations. And God often tells his people what they ought to expect. Jesus had clear expectations for his disciples when he called them (Mark 1:17), and he took care to shepherd them through their expectations about his death and resurrection (John 13–16).

As you prepare to study the Word with others, setting and communicating clear expectations can set you up for both an effective launch and ongoing success. Here are some suggestions, which you may want to consider and perhaps adapt to best fit the context in which you are leading a group.

1. **Remember the group's goal.** As I said in Chapter 1, your chief goal is *to help people know God through his Son Jesus Christ.* Although you may not always communicate this goal up front (as in the case of an investigative study with unbelievers), it should guide you as you define and communicate the expectations for the group.

2. **Establish the group's commitment level.** Think about your group. Are you reaching out to new people who don't yet know Christ or your church? You may want a low-commitment group, where they only have to show up. Are your people ready for a deeper walk with Christ but need much guidance? Then you'll likely want a moderate-commitment group, where you expect them to read and think about the passage in advance. Are you training people to study the Bible for themselves? You may want a high-commitment group, where par-

ticipants have significant homework and come with their own questions and tentative conclusions regarding the text.

3. **Give the group a clear start and end time.** People often want to know what time the meeting will begin and end so they know how to plan. You may be tempted to ask, "What time works for you?" but I don't recommend it (unless you're meeting with a key person one-on-one and you only need to work out two schedules). It's usually better to give a specific time, and—if nobody can make that time—change the time as needed. This communicates intentionality and direction.

4. **Identify starting and ending dates for the group's existence**. People may be less motivated to attend if the commitment feels endless. And with a determined end date, you'll be able to conclude the group and re-evaluate its direction. If it goes well, you could always have a six-week or six-month study, followed by another six-week or six-month study, followed by another. If it doesn't go well, becoming stagnant or ingrown, you have a designated exit ramp.

5. **Communicate your expectations.** After you've decided on the commitment level and start/end times, *communicate* this information

to the people who will attend and invite them to participate. Nothing kills the momentum of a group more than when attendees don't share a commitment level, which is what happens when a leader fails to set expectations. Such groups will decay like an unstable atomic nucleus. It is better for you to have a smaller number attending who share your expectations, than to have a larger membership with competing expectations. Your group will be better off if you maintain a clear purpose.

Depending on the parameters you chose, you may want to communicate along the following lines:

- "A few of us will get together to discuss the Bible. We'll just read a passage and talk about it. You don't have to agree with what the passage says; you just have to be honest about what it says." (In other words, you want this kind of group to be a safe space for non-Christians to attend and consider the Bible's claims without having to profess any prior loyalty to Christ or Christianity. But though you want to welcome unbelievers, you don't want to encourage a philosophical free-for-all. Therefore, you set the ground rules up front: we first figure out what the biblical author is saying to his audience; then we're free to discuss whether we agree with it or not.)

- "I'm starting a Bible study for people who want to go deeper into the Word. We'll meet every other week for 6 six months, and we'd like to have some consistency from meeting to meeting. We'll all read the passage at least once before we come so we can dive right into the discussion. Would you be interested in joining us?"

- "Our group will focus on learning how to study the Bible. We expect people to treat it like a class, with homework before each meeting."

Now as you go, keep in mind that our expectations for small-group Bible study are not like the laws of the Medes and the Persians, indelible until world's end. You can lead different kinds of groups, and even adjust the character of a group over time as best suits your people.

With the goal in mind, the commitment level established, and the dates and times proposed, you've got clear expectations for the group, and you're ready to communicate them as you recruit people to the group in earnest.

Recruitment

People often need multiple invitations before they will come. As you recruit, you can build your relationships with people and embody Christ's love to them. Let them know how much you care and how much you want them to attend. Let them know about the group's vision and how the group will help them (to figure life out, to draw closer to Christ, to learn how to study the Bible, etc.). Jesus didn't simply announce openings for disciple positions, hand out a flyer, and wait to see who would show up. He personally recruited those he wanted (Mark 1:16–20). Paul followed the same approach (Acts 13, 14, 16, 17, etc.).

Think about your first Bible study or church experience. Did you just show up on your own, or did others recruit you?

Now let me clarify that when I say *recruit*, I don't mean any of the following tactics:

- Begging
- Tricking
- Manipulating or badgering
- Coercing
- Motivating through guilt
- Promoting an artificial or purely outward commitment to the group (attending meetings without really participating)

No, by *recruit* I mean leading with vision. Winning people's hearts for the sake of Christ's mission. Building relationships and deepening godly friendships. Such recruiting is an essential part of starting a Bible study (and keeping one going).

Recruiting Is Not Necessarily Worldly

Although recruiting is often godless and manipulative, it must not be so with us. Though the world models deceptive and aggressive sales techniques, the antidote to such things is not to avoid recruiting but to do it in a Christlike way. The one who existed in the very nature of God did not consider equality with God something to be grasped (Philippians 2:5–8). He left the comfort of heaven to be with us and recruit us to himself (Matthew 1:22–23). He personally recruited his first disciples through compelling vision and relational interaction (Mark 1:16–20, John 1:35–51).

Recruiting Is Not Contrary to God's Providence

Sometimes I justify my failure to recruit people by claiming to rest in God's providence. "If God wants people to come to my Bible study, he will bring them."

Now I don't mean to imply that our efforts can generate foolproof results. God's providence *should* comfort us when things don't go as we expect — such as when we put forth our best recruiting effort and nobody comes. But consider how the Apostle Paul responded to the providence of God in his ministry:

- The Spirit of Jesus did not allow him to enter Bithynia. But instead of giving up, he pursued a different direction until the Lord made his way clear (Acts 16:7–8).

- Paul knew the sovereign Lord would bring all people before his judgment seat. Yet rather than causing him to wait passively for God's providence to work things out, Paul's belief in the coming judgment compelled him to increase his efforts to persuade people (2 Corinthians 5:10–11, 2 Timothy 4:1–2).

Recruiting Requires Self-Motivation

Time for a gut check: Do you believe Bible study is worth your time? Are you reading this book from a sense of obligation, or because the fire in your belly cannot be quenched? Have you tasted and seen the fruit of personal Bible study in knowing Jesus and becoming more like him? Are you convinced that the words of Scripture are the words of eternal life, such that you cannot stop speaking of what you have seen and heard? Until these words have gripped you, you won't be able to grip others with them.

Recruiting Is Hard Work

The task of recruiting often wages war against what we hold most dear.

Some people love simplicity and resist complexity. For example, I'd rather build something and wait for people to come. It's easier to advertise than to get to know people. It's cheaper to blanket the air waves than to connect with individuals. Time spent recruiting takes away from time I could spend accomplishing other tasks. It attacks my idol of productivity. For me, recruiting is hard work.

Some people love approval and fear rejection. They'd rather say nothing than risk disapproval. They prefer to keep to themselves rather than extend an invitation that might be declined. They assume that not trying is better than trying and failing. For such people, recruiting is hard work.

Effective recruiting requires listening to people and understanding them. It means I have to pay attention and figure out what really motivates different people. (Jesus did this when he used a fishing metaphor with fishermen in Mark 1:17.) Normally, I prefer for people to listen to *me* and understand me. I want them to do what motivates *me*. Recruiting is hard work.

Recruiting Is a Fruit of Faith and Love

When we have faith that God's Word is living and active, changing people, we will act despite our fears and, in Jesus' name, swing for the fences. When we love our neighbors in their lostness, immaturity, or foolishness, we will beg them to "come and see" the Lord who speaks words of eternal life. We will recruit them to study the Bible with us.

Recruiting Doesn't Cease after the First Meeting

Jesus never stopped recruiting his disciples to himself (John 6:66–71, 21:15–19). We haven't succeeded if we recruit people only to a single meeting. We must continue winning, persuading, challenging, and instructing. We share what God has done and what he can do further. We build deeper relationships until we, with Paul, can say, "For now we live, if you are standing fast in the Lord" (1 Thessalonians 3:8).

Without ongoing recruiting, our Bible studies are likely to fizzle. Our relationships will grow cold. Our energy and liveliness will seep out.

But what a privilege that God wants to use you and me to show the world his initiating, pursuing, and persuasive love. Let's set our expectations accordingly.

Part 2

Preparing to Lead

There's an insatiable market in today's Christian world for Bible study workbooks and leader's guides. Apparently, many people want to discuss the things of the Lord. And God has gifted some to unveil the riches of God's Word for broad audiences. Now while this is to be celebrated, we ought to consider some potential, unfortunate side effects:

- We might train people to believe the Bible on its own is not sufficient for life and godliness.

- We learn to trust the experts more than we learn to trust the inspired text.

- When lost, we never learn how to find our way through a Bible passage.

- We promote a priestly layer of "materials mediation" between people and God.

- We communicate that others should not try this at home. As if leading a Bible study is too difficult and dangerous for those without an advanced degree.

So I'm not surprised that people can be scared to lead a Bible study. They *should* be, if their idea of Bible study is limited to a workbook. Not just anyone can package up big truths for wide consumption.

But your Bible study doesn't need to be packaged for wide consumption. No book publisher knows your group members as well as you do. No one is as well-equipped to bring God's truth to *that* group of people as you are. So why not be his mouthpiece to them?

The next five chapters will equip you to prepare a fruitful Bible study discussion. In Chapter 4, we'll consider the foundational mindset for our preparation: *dependence on the Lord*. Then we'll walk through four phases in the work of preparation:

- Figure out what God has said

- Figure out how to apply what God has said

- Decide how to lead your group toward what God has said

- Consider your launching question

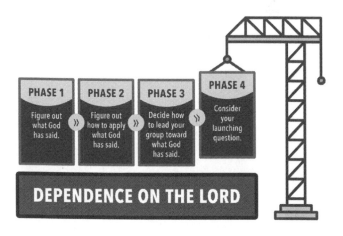

Four

Establish Your Foundational Mindset

Dependence on the Lord

Apart from Christ, we can do nothing. We'll bear no fruit unless we stay connected to the vine (John 15:4–5). Therefore, the foundational mindset for preparing a Bible study is one of dependence on the Lord. Fail to depend on him, and our preparation will not be fruitful.

If we're depending on the Lord, we will desire to pray before we begin preparing, while we prepare, and after we prepare. But prayer isn't the only way to express dependence. This chapter will focus on two additional key areas.

In the context of Bible study, we can practice dependence on God, first, by *preparing ourselves to learn* just as much as we *prepare ourselves to teach*, and second, by avoiding a common weakness among Bible teachers: manufactured profundity.

Does Your Bible Teaching Hijack Your Bible Learning?

Personal study time is costly, especially when there's a flock to shepherd.

The Scenario

You might be a teacher with lessons to prepare. You might be a mentor with disciples who need direction. You might be a parent with children who need constant nurture. You might simply be a friend with confused or inquisitive companions who have questions about Christianity.

Whatever the case, your personal Bible study time perpetually drifts toward "teaching prep" time.

You can't read a passage without envisioning how you would teach it. Your mind focuses on what might help your students. Your parental concern drives your application. Or your study consists of finding answers to your friend's latest questions.

This inclination to help others is a very good thing, and *it does not make your Bible study any less personal or acceptable to God.* As we saw in Chapter 2, application of Scripture can go in two directions: personal growth (inward) and influential leadership (outward). Many people focus on the former and exclude the latter. You, however, may have the opposite tendency.

Let Your Teaching Flow out of Your Learning

To compensate for an over-emphasis on outward application, sometimes leaders schedule designated time for personal growth. They think, *I'm going to set aside time to study the Bible so I can learn from it — not just so I can teach it.*

But these two things ought not be separated. <u>You can't teach the Bible effectively without first learning from it.</u> And your teaching ought to embody your learning. The teaching and the learning are not and cannot be exclusive to one other (as though you can do one without the other). Therefore, if your preparation to lead a Bible study does not reserve space for applying the passage to your own life, you betray a misunderstanding of how to teach.

Look at some of Paul's ministry methods:

- He committed himself to sharing not only the gospel of God, but his own life, with his people (1 Thessalonians 2:8)

- His own example was his most influential persuasion (1 Corinthians 10:31–11:1)

- His teaching affected *him* long before he expected it to affect others (Galatians 1:11–2:10)

- He taught only what he had learned. His own life — not merely his ideas — provided the model to shape his students (Philippians 4:9)

- He didn't hesitate to use both his strengths and weaknesses as illustrations of God's grace (2 Corinthians 11:16–12:10)

- He wouldn't ask someone to do something unless he had been there and done it first – and he didn't mind drawing attention to his example if it would motivate the student (2 Timothy 2:1–2, 4:1–8)

What do these things mean for our teaching? How will a complete dependence on the Lord affect the way we prepare our Bible studies?

First, please understand that you are not qualified to teach a passage of the Bible unless you have first been changed by it.

Second, don't feel guilty if your "teaching prep" time invades your "personal study" time. Your teaching prep should include personal study and application, so why not combine the tasks?

Third, when you teach other people, whether formally or informally, share how the principles have affected your life. (I'll expand on this point when I reach Preparation Phase 2.) People need more than ideas; they need role models. When God wanted to teach us, he became one of us and lived out his teaching among us. We ought to follow his example.

Unless people see how you've learned *what you teach*, your teaching will lack bite. Your principles will sound like platitudes. Your education will feel empty. Your recommendations will ring hollow. Your learnedness will lose its luster.

I've seen it happen time and again. I'm counseling someone on an issue, and truths don't click for them until I share how I've struggled with the same issue. My children respond best when they have seen that I need to grow in Christ as much as they do. My small group's application discussion hits fifth gear *after* I've shared my own failures and my hope in the grace of Christ.

I'm not saying it's easy. It's the most difficult part of my teaching prep, as it requires me to depend on Christ and not my performance.

But I've got to share my life with those I lead. My effectiveness depends upon it.

Please Don't Try to Be Profound

For aspiring Bible study leaders, the next mistake, which likewise betrays a failure to depend on the Lord, is trying to be profound. This mistake can arise from a desire to be needed or a desire to have an impact. And while a desire to have influence can be a good thing (Hebrews 5:12a, 1 Timothy 3:1), it sours when it becomes the main thing and replaces the goal of helping others to know God through his Son Jesus Christ (see Chapter 1). Therefore, when our chief passion becomes leading a profound Bible study, we ought to examine whether we have disconnected from the vine of Christ to exalt ourselves.

I remember my first study. I had persuaded two J/V football players and a skateboarder from my college freshman dorm to discuss the Bible with me. They didn't know Christ yet, and I wanted to be the one to win them to him. I knew what it felt like to be inspired in profound ways by good teachers, and I wanted others to feel the same way about me.

So I tried my hardest to impress them with my knowledge and cleverness. I came with my best alliteration, penetrating one-liners, and overconfident zeal. We met two or three times, and I gave it all I had. But all I had wasn't good enough. They lost interest and stopped showing up.

Profundity Strangles Influence

Now I don't mean to say my overzealous attempt to seize influence was the only factor in their lack of interest. I simply want to suggest that we get in trouble when we put things in the wrong order.

You teach the Bible because you want to minister to people. But people are like wet bars of soap, and you know what happens when you squeeze too hard. If your chief goal in teaching the Bible is to influence people, you may see quick results, but it won't take long for influence to morph into coercion or control. You need a better goal — one that keeps you connected to the vine.

Dependence Produces Love

This is why the foundational mindset for preparing fruitful Bible studies is to depend on the Lord. Jesus explains such godly dependence in John 15:

> I am the vine; you are the branches. Whoever abides in me and I in him, he it is that bears much fruit, for apart from me you can do nothing. (John 15:5)

While countless mystical interpretations have been offered for what it means to abide in Jesus, the context leaves little doubt:

> As the Father has loved me, so have I loved you. Abide in my love. If you keep my commandments, you will abide in my love, just as I have kept my Father's commandments and abide in his love. (John 15:9–10)

> This is my commandment, that you love one another as I have loved you. (John 15:12)

> I chose you and appointed you that you should go and bear fruit and that your fruit should abide....These things I command you, so that you will love one another. (John 15:16–17)

Jesus describes the flow of vitality and power through the following grid: The Father loves Jesus ⇨ Jesus loves his disciples ⇨ The disciples love others. The disciples get the power to love by abiding in Jesus' love. Jesus gets the power to love by abiding in the Father's love. Thus, if anyone in the chain unplugs from the sequence, he loses power, and his fruit dies. In other words, he'll fail to love.

So what does it mean to abide in Jesus? It means we abide in his love. We grab hold of it and never let it go. We remind ourselves of his love by thinking and speaking of it incessantly.

What is Jesus' love? It's not a mystical or sappy experience, but the act of laying down his life to make his servants into his friends (John 15:13–15). It's the message of the gospel.

So what does it mean to bear fruit? It means, of course, that we love others by laying down our lives for them, just as Jesus did for us.

Love Unlocks Joy

What does all this have to do with leading Bible studies?

When our aim is to be profound, we have disconnected ourselves from Jesus' love. We've turned from the message of his death for sin, and we've turned to our own need to be needed. The solution to this problem is to get reconnected to the vine, to depend on the Lord and his love.

Remember that dependence on the Lord is the foundational mindset when preparing to lead a Bible study. That's because trusting in Jesus and his love frees us to:

1. **Discover more than create.** What cleanses people is not the words we speak when we lead Bible study, but Jesus' Word to them (John 15:3). This removes the pressure of *having to create a brilliant study lesson.* We can simply discover what Jesus has already spoken in the text and then communicate that very message to others, watching *it* do the work of cleansing. Such dependence is the foundation for the first preparation phase: *Figure out what God has said.*

2. **Be honest about how the text is changing us.** As leaders, we must model not only observation and interpretation but also application. This removes the pressure of *having to appear flawless as a leader.* We don't need to project impenetrable maturity, and we can get in the muck, in appropriate ways, with the people we lead. Applying the text first to ourselves qualifies us to help apply it to others. Such dependence undergirds the second preparation phase: *Figure out how to apply what God has said.*

3. **Lay down our lives to serve.** We don't need to get other people to make us feel good. This removes the pressure of *having to evoke certain responses or outcomes.* We can simply shape our studies in a way that will serve these people at

this time, making the message of the text as clear as possible to this group. Such dependence is the basis for the third preparation phase: *Decide how to lead your group toward what God has said.*

4. **Lead people in the right direction.** We can take loving initiative with people the way Jesus did with us. This removes the pressure of *having to wait for the magic to happen.* Dependence does not mean doing nothing. Therefore, we stake our claim on the passage's main point, and we strive to lead our people interactively to that point without allowing the discussion to devolve into a free-for-all. Such dependence is the foundation for the fourth preparation phase: *Consider your launching question.*

Compared to profundity, love is not only more honoring to God; it's also a lot more fun. It reduces anxiety and produces satisfaction. "These things I have spoken to you, that my joy may be in you, and that your joy may be full" (John 15:11).

Five

Figure Out What God Has Said

Preparation Phase 1

When Bible study leaders set their hope on the Lord, they're free to discover the biblical author's message in the designated text, without feeling pressure to create a brilliant or profound study lesson. Before guiding others in such discovery, the leader must diligently observe and interpret the text according to the principles described in Chapter 2, until the biblical author's main point becomes clear.

Observe and Interpret

Instead of repeating material from Chapter 2, let me highlight how to employ those skills when preparing to lead others in a discussion of the passage.

1. **Pray at every stage of your personal study.** Remember not to disconnect yourself from the vine of Christ!

2. **Read the full text three to five times to saturate yourself in it.** You want to internalize the text, so you can more easily notice big ideas, the flow of thought, and repeated words.

3. **Pay special attention to the text's structure.**
   One of the best ways to lead a discussion is to
   go paragraph by paragraph (or stanza by stanza,
   for poetry), so you'll need a clear grasp of the
   structural divisions.[2]

4. **Figure out the main point of each paragraph**
   (or stanza). List them. Contemplate how one
   leads to the next, which leads to the next, etc.
   This process enables you to follow the author's
   train of thought. In *persuasive* texts, that train
   of thought will typically consist of a series of
   conclusions building a case. In *narrative* texts,
   the train will typically consist of a series of
   conflicts (or increasing tensions) building to
   a grand reversal (the climax) and new state of
   affairs (the resolution). In *poetic* texts, the train
   will typically consist of a series of metaphors
   and/or feelings reflecting on God's truth or
   describing an experience.[b]

5. **Keep asking and answering questions,**
   especially "Why" questions, until you can see
   how the text fits together.

6. **Write down, in a concise sentence, what you
   think is the passage's main point.** Don't
   include every detail or point made along

---

b. For more on finding the main point of persuasive, narrative, and poetic
texts, see Chapter 3 of the second edition of *Knowable Word: Helping
Ordinary People Learn to Study the Bible* (Cruciform Press, 2022).

the train of thought; most of the points are sub-points building to a bigger idea. And be careful to land on the main point and not a mere summary of the passage's content.[c] The clearer you can get on the big idea, the more likely you are to both understand and be able to communicate what God has said in this text.

7. **Now invite a good commentary or two to converse with you.** They may affirm or strengthen your main point. Or they may have additional insights into the text or corrections to your thinking which might reshape your articulation of the main point.

8. **Look back over your observations and interpretive questions,** which we discussed in Chapter 2. List or circle three to five of the most crucial observations and interpretive questions that gained you the most ground toward the author's main point. You'll use these to craft a few discussion questions for the meeting. Hang on to them for now; I'll explain the use of discussion questions in Chapter 9.

Now you can create a page of notes to take with you into the discussion. I organize my notes according to the following sections:[3]

---

c. See "How Do We Find the Main Point" in Chapter 3 of *Knowable Word: Helping Ordinary People Learn to Study the Bible* for instruction on how to convert a summary to a main point.

- **Launching question:** I'll cover this under Preparation Phase 4 (Chapter 8).

- **Main point:** Write your clear statement of the author's main point in a single sentence.

- **Supporting truths:** Write a concise outline of the text, listing verse divisions for the paragraphs/stanzas, and stating the main point for each section.

- **Connection to Christ:** Briefly state how the main point finds fulfillment in the person and/or work of Jesus Christ.

- **Observation/Interpretation questions to lead to the main point:** I will explain these in Chapter 9.

- **Application questions:** I will explain these in Chapters 6 and 9.

I recommend that your entire set of notes take up no more than a single sheet of paper. Then you'll be focused on the most important aspects of the text, and you won't have to juggle several pieces of paper while trying to lead a discussion. (You can download a template from *https://www.knowableword.com/resources.*)

I confess that getting to this point is hard work! Is it worth it?

Diligence: A Fruit of Dependence

I'm sitting in a Bible study, digging into a psalm with a group of people, when a woman bursts out, "Why are we wasting our time with all this study? Why can't we just *read*—instead of studying—and depend on the Lord?" Perhaps you had a similar question as you read through my eight recommendations for preparing and my six items to include on a note sheet.

I've bumped into proponents of this perspective with regularity. Usually, there's a claim that Bible study is too academic and disengaged from character and obedience. That relating to God should be natural and full of chemistry and compatibility. Someone once reasoned with me that toiling over Bible study would be like reading a manual about lovemaking. It deflates the personal, relational component by replacing the beloved with mere information *about* the beloved. It therefore replaces dependence on God with dependence on our study methods.

But the analogy misses the fact that this "manual" wasn't written by a disinterested third party but by the Beloved himself. The book explains how he wants to be known. Laboring to understand it is not a failure of dependence on him, but a fruit of the same.

For example, my wife occasionally sends me text messages with to-do reminders. If I fail to observe and interpret them accurately, am I expressing my love for her? If she asks me to buy milk, would she be delighted with buffalo wings? When she tells me she has a book on reserve at the library, does she want me to read it there and return it to the shelf?

I have much agreement with the people I describe above. I want to depend on the Lord too. Dependence on the Lord is the first and foundational practice for anyone who wants to lead a Bible study. And I don't think that knowledge about God should ever replace knowledge *of* God: I think we misread the book if we don't know the person behind it.

But couldn't diligence be *a sign* of dependence? When building a bunk bed, wouldn't someone express dependence by diligently following all the assembly instructions? And isn't rejection of the manual tantamount to dependence on oneself?

If you're truly depending on the Lord (the foundational mindset), you will bear the fruit of diligence as you labor to discover what God has said.

Six

Figure Out How to Apply What God Has Said

Preparation Phase 2

Once you've gained clarity on the author's main point, it's time to connect that point to the person and work of Jesus Christ and then apply it. The most important principle for preparing your application discussion is this: if you'd like to see the text change people, you'll have to prove it's changed you. Invulnerable (closed and inaccessible) leaders produce similar followers, but the beginning of wisdom is a soft heart toward the Lord (Proverbs 1:7, 9:10, 19:27).

Therefore, when preparing your Bible study, you ought to take as much time as necessary to allow the message of the text to change you. Is there something in your own life that needs to go, or that needs more attention? Has the Lord provided you an opportunity to influence your small group, your church, or your world in some way? Does the text offer you something to believe more faithfully, love more fervently, or do more eagerly?

Allowing the message of the designated text to change you isn't a nice perk or luxury; it's a prerequisite of Christlike leadership.

Beware Sanitized Hypocrisy

This should be obvious, but often isn't: we can't teach what we haven't learned. Our words are *merely* words if we can't show them by our lives. Paul's exhortation, "Be imitators of me, as I am of Christ" (1 Corinthians 11:1), would have fallen flat if he hadn't opened his life for them to see (1 Corinthians 9:1–7, 15–23; 10:32–33).

I've been challenged by this point, especially when I feel pressed for time in my teaching preparation. It's a lot faster to prepare scriptural applications for others than for myself. It's easy to ask others to change without first asking myself to change.

But the biblical word for leaders who say one thing and do another is *hypocrite*. Of course, I might avoid some of the more aggressive forms of hypocrisy: preaching integrity while robbing the church, promoting purity while secretly indulging immorality, etc. But how often do I sanitize my hypocrisy, justifying my sins of omission while passionately promoting their opposite? For example:

- Do I exhort people to confess their sins but never confess mine?

- Do I oppose pride and promote humility but refuse to let anyone see me when I'm weak?

- Do I preach about how much people need the grace of Christ but avoid revealing an inch of my own need for the grace of Christ?

- Do I urge people to love one another but believe my leadership position prevents me from having friends?

- Do I want people to be open to feedback, but avoid it myself?

Shepherds shepherd, and leaders lead. This means they go out in front and don't ask people to do anything they haven't done first. So before Jesus asked Peter to feed his lambs and die (John 21:15–19), he was the Good Shepherd who laid down his own life for the sheep (John 10:11). So also, Paul can beg the Corinthians to open wide their hearts to him after his heart was opened wide to them (2 Corinthians 6:11–13).

That kind of godly leadership requires two kinds of vulnerability:

1. When preparing to lead a study, we must allow the text to change us.

2. When leading the study, we must explain how the text has changed us.

This means I must apply the Scripture to myself before I try to apply it to anyone else. And when appropriate, I must be willing to share these lessons to give people a model for how the text can change them. After practicing these things, I'll have the credibility to suggest further applications for others.

Hear Jesus' warning against those who wouldn't do what they asked others to do:

> The scribes and the Pharisees sit on Moses' seat, so practice and observe whatever they tell you — but not what they do. For they preach, but do not practice. They tie up heavy burdens, hard to bear, and lay them on people's shoulders, but they themselves are not willing to move them with their finger. They do all their deeds to be seen by others. For they make their phylacteries broad and their fringes long, and they love the place of honor at feasts and the best seats in the synagogues and greetings in the marketplaces and being called rabbi by others. But you are not to be called rabbi, for you have one teacher, and you are all brothers. And call no man your father on earth, for you have one Father, who is in heaven. Neither be called instructors, for you have one instructor, the Christ. The greatest among you shall be your servant. Whoever exalts himself will be humbled, and whoever humbles himself will be exalted. (Matthew 23:2–12)

Those who humble themselves will be exalted. So why is such humble vulnerability so hard for us?

Why Vulnerability Is So Hard

Yesterday I arrived at one of those small but significant decision points that threaten my composure and test the limits of my willingness to be known. It came when my coworker greeted me with his usual, "How are you today?"

I wanted to reply with a perfunctory "Fine, how are you?" to complete the transaction and get on with my day, but I just couldn't do it. The truth was that I was not fine. Twice in the last week I had pled with dear friends who were departing from the faith, one into false doctrine and another into immorality. Both cases of apostasy hit me hard, and I had mourned and prayed over them, wondering what on earth God was doing.

So I cracked open the door with my colleague— "I'm pretty sad today"—and it was costly to do so. It cost a measure of self-confidence and self-respect. It cost a few minutes of my life to explain what I was sad about. It reopened the wound and renewed the pain. It sapped mental and emotional energy, as I tried to balance openness with self-control (to avoid gossip, venting, or speaking other words that wouldn't edify).

But such vulnerability is Christlike, and by faith I trust it was worth it.

Why is it so hard for us to be vulnerable with one another? Why do we struggle to lead and to teach the Scripture with transparency? Why are we more attracted to a pretense of perfection or a veneer of imperturbability? I can think of at least three kinds of reasons.[4]

Theological Reasons

I've heard pastors say they won't tell personal stories from the pulpit because it would get in the way of representing Christ. They believe that for Christ to shine brightly, they must completely get out of the way. So in private they may be perfectly happy to share about their need for grace, but their preaching focuses more on proclaiming the truth than on incarnating it.

This same sort of thinking shows up when Bible study leaders think only about how to apply the text to the group members and not to themselves. One sign of this struggle, as I mentioned earlier, is when leaders' preparation time doesn't feel devotional, and they think they need to schedule separate personal time with the Lord.

Now I have much respect for anyone who wants to "get out of the way" so people can see Christ. This desire to serve others at great cost to oneself is noble. But I think the attempt misfires, for we miss the fact that *God shows people himself by showing himself to people.* He doesn't merely declare truth; he demonstrates truth and lives it out. He became a man and perfected his power in weakness. He demonstrated his love by dying for sinners. He exposed and disgraced himself that he might lead us to glory.

And so Paul seeks to represent Jesus by placing his own life before his people, using himself as a model time and again (see Chapter 4 for a list of examples). He doesn't feel the need to "get out of the way" before he can preach Christ. He sees no conflict between preaching "nothing but Christ crucified" and opening his own life—even in the same passage (1 Corinthians 2:1–5).

Personal Reasons

Second, vulnerability might be hard for some leaders due to their personal fears or desires. Some brave souls may honestly confess pride and fear as their greatest enemies to vulnerability.

- We don't want people to think less of us

- We fear losing our position or influence

- We don't want to be a burden

- We don't want to be laughed at or seen as mistaken or needy

- Perhaps we worry that other people's perception of us is somehow an indication of God's perception of us

Whatever the exact issue, we often find our identity in something other than the finished work of Christ. We must not forget the guttural cry—"It is finished!"—of him who then bowed his head and gave up his spirit (John 19:30).

Practical Reasons

My biggest struggle, as I mentioned above, is that vulnerability is hard work. It's costly, and I'm often unwilling to pay that cost.

Make no mistake, there is an unwise sort of vulnerability that is very easy. For example, in the name of vulnerability, I could easily use my teaching role as a way to cope with my personal demons. Yet if I'm vulnerable for *my* sake — to cleanse my conscience, or even to get people to feel sorry for me — I have missed the point. Such catharsis is a foolish flavor of vulnerability that serves no one but me.

Wise vulnerability aims to serve others in meaningful ways (for example, see 2 Corinthians 11–12). And wise vulnerability takes effort. It requires forethought, self-control, and godly character. It demands unwavering confidence in Christ. For when I am weak, then I am strong (2 Corinthians 12:10).

When you prepare your Bible study, beware sanitized hypocrisy, and allow the message to change you. Only after you've done these things are you ready to serve as God's ambassador, calling others to likewise be changed by the message.

Help Your Group Consider Concentric Communities

As you prepare to help your group apply the passage, remember that personal application consists of a matrix of six boxes (see Chapter 2). You should consider the spheres of head, heart, and hands. And you can make application in any of those spheres in either of two directions: inward (personal change) or outward (helping others to consider how God may want them to change).

When you lead a group in application, however, you can also think of it in terms of concentric communities. You can help each person to consider individual application. You could also consider application to the small group (as a group), then application for the entire church or ministry of which your group is a part, and finally application for the world in which your people live.

Consider a brief example. Let's say you want to lead a group in applying the command to "love your neighbor as yourself." You could apply the command to:

- **Each group member (including ourselves):** Who are our neighbors, and how can we grow at loving those people? What obstacles prevent such love? What would improved expressions of such love look like?

- **The group itself:** How do we do at welcoming visitors, taking initiative to reach others, or recruiting? How comfortable did the last visitor or new member feel with the group?

- **The entire church community:** What

opportunities does the church have to reach its broader community? What strengths and weaknesses of the church will help or hinder its mission to love like Jesus?

- **The world:** What does the world typically believe is the best way to love someone? What cultural practices or deceptions might prove to be stumbling blocks for those who meet God's people seeking to love their neighbors?

You won't cover every one of these settings in a single Bible study, but leaders should help people consider each of these settings over time. Make sure you have variety in where you land your application each time, so you can train people to think outside themselves and to value community. I find it helpful to add one stimulating question to my page of leader's notes for each concentric community. I won't ask every question in the discussion itself, but I will be prepared to follow the flow of group discussion by pursuing application with respect to any of the possible communities.

Seven

Decide How to Lead Your Group Toward What God Has Said

Preparation Phase 3

Now that you've humbled yourself before the text, grasping the author's main point and applying it to your own life, you're ready to show others the way — even better, you're ready to help them discover the way for themselves.

Consider the main point of the passage and how to frame it in a way that will make sense to your group... Think of what's going on in their lives that might hinder or promote the truth of Christ in the passage... Consider what lies they believe and what encouragement they need to honor the Lord... Finalize your list of observation questions that will get them into the text... Anticipate what interpretive questions they may have... Craft some applications for the individuals, the group, the church or ministry, and their interactions with the world. (We discussed observation questions and interpretive questions in Chapters

2 and 5. Also see the Appendix for a sample sheet of leader's notes.)

Now, as we review this third phase of preparation, we'll see why you, as the leader of *these people* at *this time*, are more valuable to the group than a prepackaged curriculum.

Same Truth, Different Audience

Even though the author's main point is an unchanging truth, that doesn't mean you'll communicate that main point in the same way to different groups of people.

I once taught, within the space of four months, the same text in five varying settings. Although the passage's main point never changed, my presentation of it changed dramatically based on the context and audience.

My text was 2 Timothy 3:10–17. I would state the main point as follows: *We must learn from Scripture and continue in the things we've learned from Scripture.* [5] Paul's sub-points, which support his main idea, are that Scripture matters because:

1. It enables us to recognize and resist deception (2 Timothy 3:10–13).

2. It makes us wise for salvation (2 Timothy 3:15).

3. It makes us competent and equipped for every good work (2 Timothy 3:16–17).

Different audiences need different applications of the

same truths. For that reason, I wanted to frame each Bible study differently to get the most mileage with the participants.

Here's how I framed it each time—and that dictated how I advertised, introduced, and conducted the study. It gave me a different title for each discussion. It also drove which questions I asked and which set of applications we landed on.

- At a homeschooling convention, I framed the study as: *Teach your children how and why to study the Bible*.

- In an article for broad consumption, I framed it as: *My love-hate relationship with Bible study tools (and why we must learn to study the Bible itself)*.

- For the orientation of our campus ministry's summer interns, I framed it as: *Why our organization focuses on studying the Bible*.

- To help train our ministry's new staff in fundraising, I framed it as: *How the Scriptures direct our fundraising*.

- Then at my church, I framed it as: *What our church believes about the Bible*.

In all five cases, I used the same text, the same main point, and the same outline of sub-points, following the author's logic and argumentation in the text. But the overall flavor of the study changed dramatically with the audience.

I didn't invent this idea of framing a text differently to different people. Notice how two apostles can take the same text in very different directions for different audiences.

> And [Abram] believed the Lord, and [God] counted it to him as righteousness. (Genesis 15:6)

This verse is quoted three times in the New Testament, for different audiences. In each case, the main point remains intact: *God promises protection and great reward to those who take him at his word.* None of these New Testament passages violates the original intent of Genesis 15. But they re-frame the *application* of that point to reach new audiences.

- In Romans 4:1–12, Paul expects Roman believers to walk in faith, not to boast in works or religious experiences, such as circumcision.

- In Galatians 3:1–14, Paul calls Asian Gentiles to grow in Christ — and not merely come to Christ — through faith.

- In James 2:20–26, James commands Hellenistic Jews not to grow complacent in proving their faith through good deeds.

Paul and James frame their argument differently for different audiences — and so should we.

Five Things to Consider When Framing a Bible Study

How do you go about framing the study for a particular audience? How do you construct a discussion plan for a particular group of people?

1. **Don't get ahead of yourself.** The study's framing takes place during the third phase of preparing your Bible study. Don't worry about getting the framing right until *after* you've taken care to 1) understand the passage's main point, and 2) apply the main point both to yourself and those you lead. If you work on framing too soon, you may lose clarity or credibility in your leadership.

2. **Consider the group's size.** You'll prepare a Bible study differently for a small group vs. a large group. With a larger audience, questions must be more direct to keep the discussion moving. If either the question is too open-ended or the answer is too obvious, you're likely to suppress interaction. But for smaller groups, wide-open questions, such as "What stood out to you in the passage?" may work just fine.

   Thus, with a larger group, I want the passage's main point to take center stage. I'll open with it and return to it often. With a smaller group, I prefer to help the group discover the main point themselves through the discussion.

3. **Be aware of your relationship with the group.** For people he has never met, Paul—though warm—is somewhat formal (Romans 1:8–15) yet bold (Romans 15:15, 24). With close partners and key laborers, he gushes affection (1 Thessalonians 2:17–20, 3:8, 2 Timothy 2:1–8).

   Though the truth will never change, the way you pitch it may change depending on your relationship with your group. In studying 2 Timothy 3:10–17 with my church, as I noted above, I framed it as, *What We Believe About the Bible*—personal, inclusive, familiar. I'd hesitate to use the language of "what *we* believe" with a group of people I've never met; it might sound presumptuous. A better pitch for them would be *What the Bible Says About the Bible* or *What You Can Expect of the Bible*.

4. **Know the group's values and shared experience.** You'll build more credibility as a teacher if you know your people. What do they want to get out of life? What brings them together? Why are they coming to your Bible study? What events have recently affected their community? What do they value? How do they talk? What do they do when they spend time together?

When you know your group well, you'll craft a more personal and relevant Bible study, which produces higher impact and memorability.

For example, *with college students*, I try to be hip, but in an awkward sort of way (making it clear I know I'm not really hip). I do this not to get them to like me but to communicate how much I like them. It's my jam to understand these students better.

With families at church, I spend more time sharing about my family and our interactions with other families.

When I'm a guest teacher in a new place, I use that church's pew Bible, and I listen to informal conversation to find something to incorporate into the study. It's not hard to uncover a local news event, a church happening, or an individual's hope for the future. Working such things into the discussion (or into the framing of the study) makes the topic more palatable and memorable.

5. **Try different things.** The key is not to master a set of techniques but to learn to love your people. Paul models such flexible servant leadership as he preaches to different groups of people. Look at two very personal, but very different, introductions:

> "Men of Israel and you who fear God, listen. The God of this people Israel chose our fathers and made the people great during their stay in the land of Egypt…" (Acts 13:17)

> "Men of Athens, I perceive that in every way you are very religious…" (Acts 17:22)

We don't teach to feel better about ourselves, nor to earn brownie points for being truth-bearers. We do it to serve God's people and win outsiders into the Kingdom. We lead by laying down our lives and seeking to enter theirs (Mark 10:42–45). Framing your study afresh for *these people* at *this particular time* is a fabulous way to lay down your life in love.

Eight

Consider Your Launching Question

Preparation Phase 4

Your notes page for the Bible study discussion now has a well-framed main point, a brief outline of sections and sub-points, connections to Christ, and an application question for each concentric community. In addition, you've identified a few key observations and interpretations as the raw materials for questions to stimulate discussion. But you've got a glaring gap at the top of the page. What is this thing I've labeled the launching question?

Perhaps the simplest answer is that the launching question is a framing device. For most of the study, you'll have a list of possible questions to stimulate interaction, but you'll want to keep things flexible to allow the discussion to flow freely. And you can prevent that flexibility from producing chaos when you frame the discussion well from the beginning.

Begin Well

The secular world offers endless advice on presentations, public speaking, strong ledes, and captivating interpersonal communication. Some of it is quite useful. Yet, as you may have noticed, far too many Bible studies are booooring. How yours is likely to turn out begins with your first utterance. A dull and humdrum first two minutes may set the tone for the entire discussion—a swing and a miss.

If the opening is the most important part of your Bible study, how to begin well? How to grab attention while signifying what's to come? You could ask an intriguing question that leads in the right direction. Or tell a clever or heartfelt introductory story. Or make a seemingly odd suggestion and then explain its relevance. You have many options, but each promotes the same goal: hooking them early and giving them a reason to be actively engaged. This is why the final phase of your preparation will be to nail down your opening.

In his excellent *Growth Groups* training manual,[6] Colin Marshall offers his perspective on what makes for a good launching question.

As he describes it, "A launching question should be:

- **Purposeful**—introducing the main ideas or applications that will be addressed

- **Interesting**—engaging the group's attention and arousing their minds

- **Easy** — making them the experts so all can contribute early in the discussion

- **Open** — with many possible answers"

And he goes on, "There are two general types of launching questions:

- **Topical** — to raise the issues related to the goals of the study, by posing a dilemma or asking opinions

- **Textual** — to raise an issue in the text being studied which will help to unravel the whole passage."[7]

While we don't have examples in Scripture of Bible study discussions, we have plenty of examples of good introductions. They show us how God-inspired authors motivate their audiences to keep reading or listening. For example:

- In his Acts 2 sermon, Peter hooks his audience by saying, "These people aren't drunk!" and then explains the current situation by referring to Joel's prophecy.

- In Acts 17:22, Paul connects with his Athenian audience by noting that they are very religious — this draws them in to hear more about "the unknown god" they worship.

- The opening verses of letters, such as Galatians 1:1–5 or Romans 1:1–6, typically contain the letter's entire subject matter in summary form, focusing attention on the topics at hand.

- Historical narratives also typically hook readers by exposing the book's main idea early. For example, Daniel 1:1–2 narrates Yahweh's moving the kings of the earth about like chess pieces—demonstrating his authority as King of kings to both raise earthly kings up and throw them down.

By beginning a Bible study well, we give people reason to listen and take part. "But," you say, "the Bible itself is reason enough to listen and take part. We shouldn't have to try to make the Bible exciting."

And I say, "Right on." We don't have to *make* the Bible exciting, but without careful attention to the discussion's beginning, we can make it appear boring and irrelevant.

That's why the launching question is usually the last thing I do when I prepare to lead a Bible study. The goal of the launching question is not merely to capture attention; I could do that by donning a jade tutu and doing the Hokey Pokey. The goal is to unleash the text and win folks early to the main idea.

Sample Launching Questions

For those who like examples, I now spread a feast. Here's a list of sample launching questions I've used, with (hopefully) enough context for you to make sense of them. I include the main points, so you can see where I wanted the group to land by the end of the study. The launching question was my very first question to reel the people in.

For each of the following examples, the context was a church small group, meeting in my home, with a variety of adult ages and life situations among the members.

Exodus 3:7–4:17

Main point: God's agents must share God's heart for God's people, but often they don't.
Launching question: How do you normally respond to the weakness or suffering of other people?

Exodus 12:29–13:16

Main point: Future generations must know that Yahweh owns the firstborn (= everything) and remakes his creation at will.
Launching question: What is the thing you would most like to be remembered for in the future?

Romans 5:12–21

Main point: One man (and only one man) is responsible for our justification.
Launching question: Who is the most trustworthy person you've ever known? Why? And, without divulging identities, the least trustworthy? In what way were they untrustworthy?

Romans 10

Main point: Most Jews don't believe because they disobediently fail to recognize Christ as the purpose of the law.

Launching question: Have you ever used a tool for the wrong purpose? How did that work for you?

Proverbs 1:7–19

Main point: Though money is alluring (promising security and community), it is a false attraction. Only wisdom (found in fearing God and loving his instruction) can deliver such promises.

Launching question: When have you made a promise you couldn't keep? Or someone else made you a promise they couldn't keep?

Proverbs 4

Main point: Because God makes his life available through wisdom, those who turn to him have hope that anything can change.

Launching question: Have you ever felt stuck and hopeless, like something could never change? (Political elections?)

Matthew 4

Main point: As God's Son, Jesus is qualified to establish the kingdom, which changes everything.

Launching question: Has there ever been a time you failed to qualify for something? What effect did that have on your morale or aspirations?

Matthew 5:17–48

> *Main point:* To enter the kingdom of heaven, we must have the perfect righteousness of Jesus that fulfills every intent of the law.
>
> *Launching question:* Every human society has an image of the ideal good guy and the ideal bad guy. What are those ideals in our culture? What makes someone an ideal citizen? What makes someone a terribly offensive or delinquent citizen?

Conclusion

Figure out what God has said. Figure out how to apply what God has said. Decide how to lead your group toward what God has said. Consider the beginning.

These four phases will guide you to prepare fruitful Bible studies. In dependence on the Lord, they will increase your confidence in the text of Scripture and its application to both yourself and the group of people you're leading. In the next part of the book, we'll consider how to lead the meeting itself, so you can inspire others to that same confidence.

Part 3

Leading the Group

Which is worse: excessive off-topic conversation promoting unbiblical ways of thinking, or persistent pin-drop silence reinforcing uncomfortable patterns of relating? I've experienced both in small groups, and both can be among a leader's worst fears.

You can prepare the world's best Bible study on paper and still have the conversation go awry or fail to get out of the gate. But the discussion, although unscripted, needn't be uncontrollable. Although open-ended, it doesn't have to be directionless. Although interrogative, it can still be powerfully declarative.

In the next two chapters I'll address how to leverage your greatest advantage—group interaction—in the meeting itself. How do you take your careful preparation and use it to lead a discussion that stays focused on the Bible, guiding people toward deeper knowledge of God through Jesus Christ? These chapters will address issues that ought to shape the skills, character, and vision of an exceptional Bible study leader. First, I'll reflect on the all-important skill of asking good questions. Second, I'll explain how to guide the group's process of discovery without encouraging a free-for-all. Then two more chapters will discuss how to lead the people in your group toward Christ

outside of meeting times and how to grow the group
in size and maturity.

Nine
Ask Good Questions

When reading the Gospels, have you noticed how often Jesus asks questions?[8] His disciples must have been incredibly frustrated. They wanted answers; he served up another round of questions. Why? Through intentional interrogation, he often showed them that they were asking the wrong questions entirely.

Because Jesus conducted his ministry with so many inquiries, Christian faith and discernment will lead us to develop the skill of asking good questions. Such questions (and willing answers, of course) are a key part of healthy marriages, vibrant classes, joyful homes, and thriving mentorships. Likewise, good questions are the engine that propels the train of effective small group Bible studies into the station.

The most important skill for a Bible study leader to have is that of asking good questions. Questions are the fuse to ignite the explosives of interaction. Questions are the trigger to fire the ammunition of interaction. Questions are the pistol to signal the sprint of interaction. And questions are the key to wind the gears of interaction.

Do you have any questions?

Perhaps you've been in a Bible study with a skilled and wise leader, whose questions guided the group through the critical parts of a passage. You may not even remember these questions, since good questions are almost invisible. These are not the clever, witty, eloquent questions of the orator or debater. They don't draw attention to themselves. But without them, the group would function like a legs-up turtle.

Bad questions, on the other hand, are as subtle as a fire alarm. Instead of encouraging discussion, they shut it down. They interrupt the flow of dialogue and generate silence, while the leader squirms and the group members wonder what's for dinner.

What is the difference between a good question and a bad one? What are some characteristics of good questions? We will consider some general principles before exploring examples for each of the main steps of the OIA method.[9]

Six Characteristics of a Good Small Group Question

A bad question is one reason for lingering *silence in a small group Bible study*. So, for small group leaders, it is worth our time to think about what makes a good question. In my experience, good questions in small groups share these six qualities.

1. **A good question is asked in a natural order.**
   What is true in one-on-one conversations is also

true in small groups: accelerating too quickly makes things awkward. Learning and respecting the natural progression of questions is a concrete way for leaders to love their group members.

Questions should generally move from easy to difficult and from objective to personal. It is also usually advisable to ask questions that *observe* or *interpret* the text before moving to questions that *apply* the text.

2. **A good question is honest.** Having studied the Bible passage in depth before the meeting, a leader should have a point of view and a direction in which he or she wishes to lead the conversation. However, the best questions are asked in humility, understanding that even the most studied Christians have much to learn from others.

When we ask simplistic fill-in-the-blank or guess-what-I'm-thinking questions, we fail to invite *interaction*. These questions rarely supply enough oxygen to sustain a conversation.

3. **A good question is tethered to the text.** There are certainly times to probe our friends' thoughts, experiences, and feelings. After all, our group members' backgrounds and perspectives are part of what makes small groups so valuable. But within a small group Bible study, discussion should flow from the Scriptures.

If the purpose of our small group is to study the Bible, we should *ask questions about the Bible*. Our human tendency is to look away from Scripture, so many of our questions must gently remind our friends to look back at the text.

Application questions are the most personal and individual questions we can ask, but even these should originate in the text. Once we've talked through *observations* and *interpreted* the passage as a group, the *author's main point* should drive all *application* questions.

4. **A good question is understandable.** When we are excited about a Bible passage, it is easy to get carried away when writing questions. We must break our questions down into small, manageable steps.

    A good question should not be too long. It should not introduce fancy concepts or big words. Usually, it should not consist of multiple parts. To be understandable, a good question should also be concise and clear, asking people to consider something specific. If our friends can't understand what we're asking, we've little chance of a good discussion.

5. **A good question is purposeful.** When putting notes together for a meeting, a leader should have a defined plan. A major component of that plan ought to be the passage's main point, and

the leader can design a *question plan* to help the group gather the information required to arrive at that destination.

This means some interesting features of the passage may not make it into the discussion. With a limited amount of time, a leader needs to choose questions carefully.

6. **A good question is prayerfully considered.**
As leaders, we should *pray* about all aspects of our Bible study meetings. This includes our questions and the conversations they spark.

A key ingredient of planning our questions is *considering possible responses*. If we envision the answers, we can evaluate the quality of our inquiries and anticipate the need to rephrase or follow up in a particular way. And the better we *know our small group members*, the better we'll be able to predict how our questions will land on them.

Planning helpful questions is slow, difficult work and it takes time to get better. But it's worth it—for the good of our meetings and the growth of our friends. Now let's consider how to improve at asking questions at each stage of OIA Bible study.

Observation

The foundation of any Bible study lies with careful observation of the text. This is no less true for group study than it is for individual study. So how do we ask good observation questions in a group setting? Observation questions are especially easy to present as fill-in-the-blank or guess-what-I'm-thinking questions.

Let's take Acts 19:1–10 as a sample passage. Imagine you are preparing to lead a discussion on it, and you want to draw people out by drawing them into the text. Your questions will make all the difference.

Bad observation questions:

1. What baptism did the Ephesian disciples receive?
2. What was the first thing Paul did when he arrived in Ephesus?
3. When did Paul move to the hall of Tyrannus?

Good observation questions:

1. What experience of Christianity did the Ephesian disciples have before Paul arrived?
2. How does Paul interact with the Ephesian disciples?
3. How is the passage structured?

Do you see the difference? Though the bad questions require observations for answers, they do not stimulate further dialogue. They focus on a single detail, so the group members serve only to fill in the blanks left by the leader, who diligently steers clear of the conversation highway. While this approach offers a safe and easy way to create an appearance of participation, it also is not conducive to the powerful, spontaneous, and unpredictable work of the Spirit in the minds and hearts of others.

The good observation questions above, however, encourage meaningful discussion and interaction, while remaining tethered to the text, drawing out specific observations. They do this by having more than a single right answer. They are therefore more open-ended, enabling group members to pick up on the important features of a passage and not get stuck on the smaller details. These questions simultaneously engage the group and open the door to interpretation.

Interpretation

"But who do you say that I am?" (Luke 9:20) This piercing question follows a simple observation question, "Who do the crowds say that I am?" Jesus requires his disciples to consider the popular answers (John the Baptist, Elijah, one of the prophets of old) along with the witness of his teaching and life. He then presses them to make sense of their observations—to interpret them.

Interpretation questions provide an indispensable turning point for small group discussions. Though we must observe well, we must not stop there. Wise leaders challenge people to make sense of observation through vibrant interpretation. Thus, once you get the raw material of the text on the table through good observation questions, you are ready to help the group interpret.

Working Backwards

The most helpful way to develop good interpretation questions is to *work backwards*. Plant your flag on the main point of the passage and review the trail you hiked to get there.

- Which observations were most significant?
- Which questions directed me to the main point?
- Which questions were good but tangential?
- How does the argument of the passage flow from beginning to end?
- Which highlights will best serve the group?

Having retraced your steps, you can develop questions that will lead you back to the flag, this time with your group in tow.

Case Study

When I was preparing to lead my small group in a study of 1 Thessalonians 1, I stated the main point of the passage this way in my notes:

> *Be encouraged that the gospel came to you in power and that your faith in God has gone forth widely.*

How did I structure my questions to guide the group toward this idea? Here's the outline of the study.

First Thessalonians 1

1 Paul, Silvanus, and Timothy, to the church of the Thessalonians in God the Father and the Lord Jesus Christ: Grace to you and peace.

2 We give thanks to God always for all of you, constantly mentioning you in our prayers,

3 remembering before our God and Father your work of faith and labor of love and steadfastness of hope in our Lord Jesus Christ.

4 For we know, brothers loved by God, that he has chosen you,

5 because our gospel came to you not only in word, but also in power and in the Holy Spirit and with full conviction. You know what kind of men we proved to be among you for your sake.

6 And you became imitators of us and of the Lord, for you received the word in much affliction, with the joy of the Holy Spirit,

7 so that you became an example to all the believers in Macedonia and in Achaia.

8 For not only has the word of the Lord sounded forth from you in Macedonia and Achaia, but your faith in God has gone forth everywhere, so that we need not say anything.

9 For they themselves report concerning us the kind of reception we had among you, and how you turned to God from idols to serve the living and true God,

10 and to wait for his Son from heaven, whom he raised from the dead, Jesus who delivers us from the wrath to come.

1. Launching question: Can anyone tell us about an experience you've had sharing your testimony of coming to faith in Christ? (We covered launching questions in Chapter 8.)

2. Give background on the Thessalonian church. It was a young church!

3. What do you observe about Paul's thanksgiving in verses 2–3?
   Follow-up: What's significant about the items Paul mentions?

4. What evidence does Paul give that God has chosen the Thessalonians?
   Follow-up: Does the power and conviction in verse 5 refer to Paul or the Thessalonians? How do you know?

5. Why does Paul mention God's choice?

6. Note that Paul is speaking of the Thessalonians' experience chronologically.

7. What happened to the Thessalonians after the gospel came to them? (See verses 6–7.)
   Follow-up: What is the difference between the way Paul uses imitator *and* example?

8. What is significant about the locations Paul mentions? (See verses 7–8.)

9. What were people saying about the Thessalonians? Why does Paul highlight these things?

10. The main verbs in verse 9–10 are *turn*, *serve*, and *wait*. How are these actions important for young Christians?
    Follow-up: How are these actions important for more mature Christians?

11. Does Paul intend verses 9–10 to be a summary of the Christian life? How do you know?

12. How does the gospel relate to verses 9–10?
    Follow-up: How do verses 2–8 relate to verses 9–10?

13. What is Paul's main point in writing Chapter 1? How do you know?

14. What implications does this have for us? What implications does this have for our work making disciples? (This question moves into application, which we'll cover in the next section.)

Let me connect this question plan to the six characteristics I outlined at the start of the chapter.

- **Natural order**—While the launching question is personal, none of the other questions get personal until the end. I also try to ask easier, *observational questions* (like questions 3 and 4) before harder, *interpretive questions* (like questions 5, 8, or 11).

- **Honest**—While I studied this passage quite a bit, I knew that others in my group had

much to teach me. So I wanted my questions
to be open and inviting (like the follow-up to
question 3 and questions 8 and 10). I also avoid
fill-in-the-blank questions—it's actually for
this reason that I simply state some observations (see #6 above) instead of asking about
them. I don't want my group to feel they must
read my mind.

- **Tethered to the text**—In many of the questions,
  I use specific language from the passage or verse
  numbers. In other places, when I ask, How
  do you know?, that is my effort to direct my
  friends back to the Bible for their reasoning. I
  try to leave room for people to speak from
  their different perspectives and experiences
  (questions 10, 12, and 14). But ideally all such
  discussion will spring from the words of God.

- **Understandable**—I tried to avoid long or
  complicated questions. My longest question
  above is question 10, and I would ask this twice
  before inviting responses.

- **Purposeful**—When putting this study plan
  together, I wrote down the *main point* of the
  passage and then wrote the questions to lead
  my group toward that conclusion. My hope
  was that when I asked question 13, my group
  would have a solid answer.

- **Prayerfully considered**—In my planning I try

to imagine the responses that each question could provoke. If the question is ambiguous or unclear, I reworked it with more focus. This led to several inquiries with immediate follow-ups prepared.

Preparing good questions is time-consuming, demanding work.

Tips for Your Own Interpretation Questions

Here are some closing suggestions for asking good interpretation questions.

1. **Prepare, but be flexible**. By all means, prepare well. Study, pray, and trust God as you prepare notes to guide the discussion. *But be flexible as well*. Multiple paths of observation can lead to the same main point. Remind the group (and yourself!) that you are fallible, and they may correct or adjust your interpretation if they can prove it from the text. You may have even missed the passage's main point and landed on a sub-point! Don't dismiss unexpected responses. Push your group's collective nose back into the text, and if they see something you didn't, be ready to learn and rejoice. This is part of the beauty of studying the Bible in a group.

2. **Ask honest questions.** I've mentioned it before, but it bears repeating. Make sure that

your questions are offered in a spirit of honest inquiry. *Do you really want to know how your group interprets the passage, or are you just waiting for them to catch up and agree with you?* Be curious. Seek the truth. Remember that the Holy Spirit gives understanding in different measures and at different times. When you ask a "What did he mean?" question, be ready to listen for any sensible interpretation, not only for confirmation of your own conclusions.

3. **Take one step at a time**. Find the meaning of one stanza or paragraph and move on. You don't have to survey the entire passage before discussing the component pieces. The themes from each paragraph usually swirl together in the same current to bring the main point to shore.

4. **Avoid asking, "What does this mean to you?"** Since God's truth lies in the text and not (naturally) in our hearts, we can extinguish this tricky little flame for good.

In the next chapter, we'll consider further strategies for facilitating conversation in the moment and addressing the many situations that can seem to go wrong.

Application

Welcome to the most uncomfortable part of your Bible study. Regardless of how energetic the discussion has been, getting personal will be hard work. Your group may float on the momentum of observation and interpretation like a shiny soap-bubble on a breezy spring day, yet that bubble can pop as soon as you transition to application. Impersonal abstraction will offer no further covering. You're asking people to reshape their thinking and their lives according to the Word of God, and such requests normally feel uncomfortable.

But don't shun the discomfort! When you discuss the work of God to conform his people to the image of Christ, any tension you feel is evidence of progress. When you lead your group through the awkwardness, your courage will be infectious.

Observation and interpretation questions tend to flow naturally together (see my sample plan above for 1 Thessalonians 1, where I alternate these types of questions). But more often than not, a small group discussion will have a clear point of transition out of O and I, and into A. Here are some ideas for managing that transition.

Lead the Group in Application

1. **First apply the text to yourself.** As discussed in Phase 2 for preparing a Bible study (see Chapter 6), a leader who hasn't already made personal application from the text is like an emaciated chef, an unkempt barber, or a disheveled tailor. If the text hasn't changed you, you'll have little capital with which to invest in others'

change. In fact, the areas where God's Word has most powerfully affected you will likely be the ones that stand out the most to your group. So build personal application into your preparation, and come to the meeting prepared to share whatever would be appropriate to share. However, being prepared to share your personal application doesn't necessarily mean that sharing that application is your best first move in the discussion. Therefore…

2. **Start with a general question.** In my small group, I usually transition to application with a generic, open-ended question: "How can we apply this text?" Or perhaps, "What difference are these truths going to make to us this week?" On this fishing trip, I wait five seconds before cutting bait. I'm looking for any pointed, clear work of the Spirit, because sometimes God has already granted a group member conviction and insight for change. I don't want to bottle that up, but to allow room for spontaneous eruptions of confession and grace-dependent plans to change.

3. **Then ask more specific questions.** If your group members don't respond to big, broad questions, they may need help to consider specific applications. To stimulate your preparation, consider the two directions and the three spheres of application from Chapter 2.

Additionally, consider applications for individuals, as well as for the group and the church (or ministry) as a whole. You won't have time to touch on every area of application every week, but make sure that you balance the categories over the weeks and months so the group doesn't list too much in one direction.

Case Study

Consider my Bible study, mentioned above, in 1 Thessalonians 1, where I had the following main point in mind:

Be encouraged that the gospel came to you in power and that your faith in God has gone forth widely.

Here are some potential application questions that flow from this main point:

- Two general questions to transition into application (#14 from the question plan above): What implications does this main point have for us? What implications does this have for our work making disciples?

- Getting more specific:
  - *How is our situation similar to that of the Thessalonians? How is it different?*
  - *How does reflecting on the gospel coming to you encourage you?*

- *What do you wish others would say about your faith?*

- *What are some practical ways we can make the Holy Spirit's powerful work through the gospel in us more visible to others? What are some things that tend to keep that work hidden from view?*

- *How have you seen the faith of our church community make an impact on our town or neighborhood? Whom can you encourage, by telling them of the impact you have witnessed?*

- *How would we like to see the church's reputation for faith impact our town or neighborhood still more?*

- *How have you seen the faith of other people or Christian fellowships impact their communities? Whom can you encourage, by telling them of the impact you have witnessed?*

- *How can we ensure our continued conviction in the gospel, that it may come with power and in the Holy Spirit?*

Tips for Your Own Application Questions

Here are some closing suggestions for asking good application questions.

1. **Questions belong to you; conviction belongs to the Holy Spirit.** By all means, study, think,

and pray in your preparation. But remember you cannot convict sinners of their sin. The Holy Spirit holds that job. Your job is to ask questions that lead to applications of the text and to share how God has changed you through this study. You must labor in faith, knowing that you can plant or water, but that God causes the growth (1 Corinthians 3:5–9).

2. **Be specific and personal in your questions.** As the members of your group get to know each other, you will start to know where others battle against sin. So, as the moment allows, you can ask specific application questions that tap into the group's shared history. "Jane, a few weeks ago you mentioned that you often don't know how to offer hope to your coworkers. Can you think of a way to bring the truth from tonight's passage to anyone specifically?" Or (if calling on Jane might cause undue pressure), "can anyone suggest how this passage might help in situations like Jane's?" Be very sensitive to personalities and confidences but leverage this great benefit of a small group: giving and receiving help in targeted, personal, and specific ways.

3. **Connect your application to Jesus.** Too often Christians leave Bible studies in a rush of grit and determination, or a crash of despondence and despair, rather than a dependence on God's

grace. A burst of adrenaline may enable you to push a car for a few feet, but it's no way to cross the country. And a persistent introspective defeatism reflects a conviction that power comes from within, when it really comes from above. We need Jesus' life and death for us at all times, for strength to obey and for forgiveness when we fail. And since you're leading this group, this grace must reside deep in your heart so you can guard your friends against either the let's-go-do-this-woo-hoo, or the nobody-can-do-this-boo-hoo, application fever.

Preparing to Ask Good Questions

Though some of your work to craft discussion questions will take place during your preparation before the meeting, most of the work of asking questions will take place on the fly during the meeting. The previous sections may guide you as you learn this skill, but as a Bible study leader, it is a skill you must *internalize*. That comes with practice, so there's no better way to develop the skill than simply to do it a lot.

When you're first learning the skill, you may want to take a lengthy list of pre-written questions into the meeting. But as you mature as a leader, you'll want to foster free-flowing, natural conversation more than predetermined, dialogical programming. So find the courage to go off-script from time to time, to pull on those threads the Holy Spirit has sewn into your people's hearts and minds.

After you have gained some experience, eventually your preparation may consist of writing down a launching question, three to five discussion-starting observation and interpretation questions, along with a specific application question for each concentric community your people are part of. (Don't forget about the Appendix to this book, which you may find helpful here.) Then the majority of the discussion takes place when you simply ask *follow-up* questions based on what people say.

Taking the time to memorize a few stock questions may equip you to foster further interaction in any Bible study discussion:

- "Where exactly do you see that in the text?"
- "Great observation; why do you think he says it that way?"
- "What significance does that have in the author's train of thought?"
- "How does that fit with what comes right before and after?"
- "If someone really grasped what this is saying, how would their marriage and family life, personal finances, relationships, thought life, etc. be any different?"

Anyone who wishes to harness the power of interaction to lead a vibrant Bible study must ask good questions and listen carefully in order to ask appropriate follow-up questions. As these skills become instinctive, you'll be able to guide nearly any group's process of discovery.

Ten

Guide the Process of Discovery

Remember—you have chosen to lead a particular group of people in a specific study of God's Word so you can harness the power of interaction to help them know God through his Son, Jesus Christ. In this chapter, we'll consider a variety of topics to help you achieve these things without losing control of the discussion altogether.

Different People are... Different

I would never accuse my friend Kevin of being a people person (he may even agree with me!), but his humanitarian insight nearly knocked my socks off.

We sat in a coffee shop, just days before our college graduation. Kevin had studied mechanical engineering and not philosophy, but that didn't prevent him from ponderous reflection as he approached one of life's major milestones. Although he had locked himself in a computer lab for the past four years and had only just come up for air, he was able to answer my question with a deliberate clarity I didn't expect.

"What is the most helpful thing you've learned in college?" I asked him.

"People are so interesting. Each one is different."

With our schoolwork behind us, we could spend a lazy afternoon unpacking this profound truth together. Kevin shared his regrets: not making more time for friends. I shared mine: not being quicker to see how the differences among people were very good. We committed ourselves to praising God for making so many people so different.

Leading Bible Study

Decades later, this conversation still haunts me when I find myself getting annoyed by people who aren't like me. Especially people who slow me down. Especially when I'm doing something important like leading a Bible study. (Yes, I still have work to do in this area...)

People are different. Their motives are different. Their challenges, experiences, and dreams are different. The Lord's work in each one is different, and the pace of each person's spiritual growth is different.

Some people attend a Bible study—knowing full well it is a *discussion* group—and yet never say a word. Others come and never stop talking. And some seem to forget that the goal is to study the Bible, not to air personal opinions.

Through it all, your mission as a Bible study leader remains the same:

> Preach the word; be ready in season and out
> of season; reprove, rebuke, and exhort, with
> complete patience and teaching. (2 Timothy 4:2)

Complete patience means I should not mind that people are different. *Complete teaching* means my goal for each person remains the same—I will strive to preach Christ and him crucified (1 Corinthians 2:2), and I will make every effort to see that nobody fails to obtain the grace of God (Hebrews 12:15).

Seeing the Opportunities

When you find yourself getting impatient with the quirks of others, it may be helpful to remember the opportunities created by our differences:

- **The unbeliever** may help your group ask questions it never would have considered on its own.

- **The aggressive atheist** may tie his own noose if he's not willing to allow the text to speak before he tries to contradict it. And in so doing, he may strengthen the faith of young Christians.

- **The silent introvert** may be the most thoughtful and considerate attendee, always ready to listen to others and process the material deeply.

- **The tenure-seeking lecturer** may bring some helpful knowledge of theology or historical background to the table.

- **The off-topic questioner** may care more about application than you do.
- **The critical nitpicker** may help you become a better leader.
- **The spontaneous emoter** may be your best recruiter and may prevent the Bible study from becoming a purely academic exercise.
- **The invulnerable thinker** may be able to develop the best strategy for growing the group.

Truth is singular; people are plural. Good leaders learn to connect the two. Without compromise, and with complete patience.

Eight Effects of a Wise Leader's Words

In any meeting focused primarily on discussion, people's differences quickly become apparent, and that can get messy. It's easy to find good advice for moderating the messiness—such as how to confront conversation hijackers or redirect discussion detours—so I won't repeat it here.[10] Instead, I'd like to reflect on the effects of wise words, because the wisdom of God will equip you to adapt to any circumstances—even if you haven't yet read the latest advice on your particular situation.

> The mouth of the righteous is a fountain of life,
> but the mouth of the wicked conceals violence.
> (Proverbs 10:11)

> The lips of the righteous feed many, but fools die
> for lack of sense. (Proverbs 10:21)

God's righteous wisdom is a great blessing for his people, for those with such wisdom on their lips "feed many." In fact, I would rather attend one Bible study led by a Christlike sage whose godliness disinfects any mess, than a hundred Bible studies led by a know-it-all or by someone who has perfected all the latest communication techniques. The wisdom of God demands we not only do wise things (Proverbs 1:2–3) but also become wise people (Proverbs 1:4–6). Thankfully, the Lord has made the evidence of such wisdom easily observable so we can search it out and make it our own.

1. Wise Words Deliver

With his mouth the godless man would destroy his neighbor,
but by knowledge the righteous are delivered.
(Proverbs 11:9)

Wise leaders communicate knowledge that delivers—repentance and faith take root, conflict resolves, lives change. Those with no divine commission need only their mouths to destroy. But those who represent the creator of heaven and earth have been given a more productive job.

2. Wise Words Delight

To make an apt answer is a joy to a man, and a word in season,
how good it is! (Proverbs 15:23)[d]

---

d. See also Proverbs 16:24, 24:24–26, 25:25

When wise leaders speak, people rejoice. Words fit for a particular season in someone's life can't be programmed; they simply flow from a heart that is conditioned to consider others' needs more than its own.

3. Wise Words Gladden

Anxiety in a man's heart weighs him down, but a good word makes him glad. (Proverbs 12:25)

If you want those you lead to arrive at delight, as we just mentioned, at times you may need to help them get there. The first step is to encourage them through their dark moments. This "good word" that gladdens has very little to do with getting the sentiments exactly right. It has everything to do with listening, asking questions, and letting yourself feel what they feel. Often, the good news comes when they simply find they don't have to suffer and groan alone (Romans 8:22–27).

4. Wise Words Heal

Gracious words are like a honeycomb, sweetness to the soul and health to the body. (Proverbs 16:24.)

Wise leaders speak grace that not only rescues from sin but also directs toward righteousness. Such sweetness brings true healing to body and soul. Sometimes we think "healing" has to involve "the process of speaking every angry thought you've had toward the person who offended you in order to get closure." But the grace of true spiritual healing stands in stark contrast to such violent sword thrusts (Proverbs 12:18).

5. Wise Words Defuse

A soft answer turns away wrath, but a harsh word stirs up anger. (Proverbs 15:1)

When a wise leader enters a heated conversation, tempers dissipate and people who may feel misunderstood learn to focus more on understanding others than on being understood themselves. A soft answer involves not only a kind and patient tone but also a skill with letting one's reasonableness be known to everyone (Philippians 4:5). A wise teacher won't begin refuting an opposing viewpoint until the opponent agrees that his position has been represented fairly and without false generalization.

6. Wise Words Persuade

The wise of heart is called discerning, and sweetness of speech increases persuasiveness. (Proverbs 16:21)[e]

Wise leaders have a reputation for distinguishing truth from error. People in need of help seek them out and ask for their opinions. Such leaders can often pinpoint main ideas, use accurate labels, predict the likely consequences of an action, and recommend a wise course of action. And hungry souls find such speech extraordinarily sweet.

7. Wise Words Inspire

The tongue of the wise commends knowledge, but the mouths of fools pour out folly. (Proverbs 15:2)[f]

---

e. See also Proverbs 16:23
f. See also Proverbs 15:7.

When good leaders adorn the truth with beauty (words that are seasonal, good, gracious, soft, and persuasive), people discover a thirst they didn't know they had. The knowledge of God becomes more desirable, and folly looks not only foolish but also repulsive.

8. Wise Words Influence

Righteous lips are the delight of a king, and he loves him who speaks what is right. (Proverbs 16:13)

Sometimes we worry about what people think of us, and we should repent. But other times we don't think about it enough, and we should likewise repent. People can love you for the wrong reasons, but they can also love you for the right reasons. The problem is not with the love but with the reasons. Do they think of you as someone who speaks what is right? Do people follow your leadership because they have to, or because they want to?

By all means, please do learn good techniques for leading Bible study discussions. But more importantly, please gain lips of wisdom.

Three Disciplines to Develop Wise Speech

Perhaps you've tasted and seen the effects of a wise leader's words, and you want to be that kind of leader. You want to learn to speak words that deliver, delight, gladden, and heal. You'd like to be able to defuse, persuade, inspire, and influence. You can picture leading such Bible studies, but you don't know how to move in that direction. You see the potential, but you don't know how to realize it.

You're not alone, and you don't have to feel stuck. Proverbs describes not only the effects of wise words, but the practices that will help you produce those effects. And while Proverbs has quite a bit to say about the wise leader, I have found the following three practices to be particularly helpful with leading Bible studies. Practicing these three disciplines will, by God's grace, give you something to offer your people during the meeting. "The lips of the righteous feed many" (Proverbs 10:21).

1. Listen More Than You Speak

If one gives an answer before he hears, it is his folly and shame. (Proverbs 18:13)[g]

When leading Bible studies, your goals should be, first, to hear others, and second, to give an answer. Reverse the order, and you're on the way to shameful folly.

What does this mean? What does it look like to hear before giving an answer?

- You care more about winning people than about being right.

- You want to know what other people think more than you want them to know what you think (even when you're the leader).

---

g. See also Proverbs 18:2.

- You learn how to ask good observation, interpretation, and application questions that stimulate discussion and don't shut it down.

- You create a group culture where crazy, even false, ideas can be freely spoken. (Please note: This doesn't mean you create a culture where crazy, even false, ideas are accepted. Loving people doesn't mean compromising the truth. At the same time, loving the truth doesn't require you to feel threatened by questions or objections.

- You ask open-ended questions. This means you avoid questions that can be answered with just a yes or a no, or questions that have only one correct answer. Questions like this are not discussion questions—they're quizzes.

- You pay attention to what people say.

- You reflect what you hear people say, rephrasing their comments in your own words. This demonstrates that you understand the substance of what they were saying.

- You don't answer every question yourself but toss questions back out to the group—"What does everyone else think about that?"

2. Draw Others Out

The purpose in a man's heart is like deep water, but a man of understanding will draw it out. (Proverbs 20:5)

Listening is good. It's an important first step. But if

that's all you do, it's more like a support group than a Bible study. People are like wells, and your goal is to lower the bucket and scoop out their purposes. You want to help them understand God's word and themselves better than they did before. Once they do, change becomes possible.

Let me illustrate. One person leads a Bible study on Romans 3:9–20 and teaches the material well. She observes the text skillfully and gets people looking up all the Old Testament quotes. She shows how these passages about Israel's enemies are used by Paul to describe Israel itself. The leader communicates a clear doctrine of human depravity, and she challenges people to trust in Christ and not themselves. They listen eagerly, happy to learn and grow.

Another person leads a study on the same passage, but does so through the use of thoughtful questions, careful listening, and stimulating follow-up questions. She covers the same content as the other leader, and she gets people talking about the topic of depravity on their own. One person mentions an obnoxious family member, and the leader asks her how that relationship has colored her view of the world. Another person challenges the doctrine of depravity, and the leader—who doesn't jump on the objector with immediate correction—asks more questions to understand why it's so hard to swallow. Another participant confesses feelings of guilt whenever the topic of sin arises, and the leader sensitively coaxes further context-appropriate detail from her.

When you actually understand *why* people think what they think, you're in the best position to convince them to think something else. When you understand *why* people respond the way they do, you'll be able to connect the dots for them so they can repent and choose different responses in the future. If you don't scoop out the purposes in their hearts, you'll end up with a group that agrees with what you've taught but doesn't understand how to make specific changes to their lives. The result? Very little change in their lives.

3. Sweeten Your Speech

The wise of heart is called discerning, and sweetness of speech increases persuasiveness. (Proverbs 16:21)

If you listen and draw others out, the time will come for you to speak. And you won't have to say much, because your words will weigh more for all your listening and investigation. But it's a good time to remind yourself that our words still matter.

When the time comes for you to speak, it's not a good time to criticize people who aren't in the room. "I can't believe how wrong all those Arminians/Calvinists/Baptists/Presbyterians are…"

It's also never a good time to scold a participant, belittle one who is in error, or ignite a quarrel.

Instead, you have an opportunity here. An opportunity to woo, persuade, and build trust. You get there by sweetening your speech. Give them reason to trust you and lower their defenses.

During a Bible study:

- "Other translations say…" is better than "You should get a more literal translation."
- "I can see what you're saying, but have you considered…?" is better than "I disagree."
- "That's a good question for another time. For now, what does the passage say" is better than "Please don't go off-topic."

These are not avoidance tactics, smooth-talking, or political spin. This is the wise stimulation of productive interaction through sweet, persuasive, and winsome ministry.

Keep the Context Front and Center

In the space of one week, I read some amazing things in the *New York Times*:

The president's announcement was the first official confirmation of his death.

They were disappointed, frankly, that I didn't have some breakthrough.

She was two months pregnant.

Thousands of people attended hundreds of enrollment events around the country at public libraries, churches, shopping malls, community colleges, clinics, hospitals and other sites.[11]

Are these lines as amazing to you as they were to me? No?

The Problem

All these quotes come from a single publication with a single editorial board. But they also come from a variety of articles, written by different journalists, spread out over a few days. Each article had a different topic, designed for a different column, reporting on a different news story. So, naturally, they don't mean much of anything on their own. You need the context for each one to make sense.

Do you read the Bible like this? Do you find a remarkable sentence or two here and there, memorize them, and base your hope on them? You don't read anything else this way. Not newspapers or novels. Not letters or emails, blogs or textbooks. Sure, sometimes you'll scan. Other times you'll highlight key conclusions you want to remember. But you won't limit your reading to isolated sentences.

Do you teach the Bible like this? Do you string together verses to make a point? It's fine to do so, as long as you're not doing violence to what those verses mean in context. Paul does it in Romans 3:10–18, David does it in 1 Chronicles 16:7–36, and Jonah does it in Jonah

2:1–9. But Satan can quote isolated statements from the Bible in support of evil intentions (Matthew 4:6). Plenty of folks today likewise excel at sampling Bible verses to mix some truth in with catastrophic error.

The Challenge of Bible Studies

In a Bible study meeting, you may have thirty to ninety minutes to dive into a particular text. You'll look at the details, ask many specific questions, and try to make particular applications. As you work on a small portion of text, how do you keep the big picture (the context) front and center? How do you prevent the group from moving from one isolated text to another, week after week, without ever fitting them together?

A Proposed Solution

These suggestions are not the only ones you could follow, but they summarize what I've found most helpful.

1. **Do a good book overview.** When leading a study through a book of the Bible, I always dedicate the first meeting to a book overview.[h] The overview gives us clarity on the historical context: author, audience, occasion, and structure. But more importantly, it enables us to discuss the entire book's main point. For

---

h. See Chapter 2 of *Knowable Word*, specifically the sections titled "The Book Overview Process" and "Genesis 1:1–2:3," for more help with preparing a book overview.

example, in my church small group studying Romans, our book overview led us to a pretty clear main point: Paul wants to preach the gospel to those who are in Rome (see Romans 1:15–17).

2. **Remind the group of where you've been**. Each week, I make sure to summarize the text's argument over the last few chapters — or ask someone else to summarize it for us. This enables us to situate the present text within the book's flow of thought. For example, our study of Romans 3:9–20 came as the climax to Paul's argument that began in Romans 1:18. Before tackling Romans 3:9–20, we briefly reviewed the section up to that point: God's wrath is revealed against the immoral (Romans 1:18–32), God's wrath is against the moral (Romans 2:1–16), and God's wrath is against the outwardly religious (Romans 2:17–3:8).

3. **Make sure to grasp the passage's main point**. By definition, focusing on the main point enables you to focus on what God considers most important. Incidentally, it also helps you not to get lost in the sea of sub-points and minutiae that so easily commandeer your attention. As you keep main points front and center, you'll decrease the likelihood of missing the context.

4. **Connect each passage to the book's main point.** Every week, as we studied a new section

of Romans, we asked, "How does Paul preach the gospel (good news) in this passage?" The key here is to take the passage's main point and show how it advances the book's main point. Of course, in Romans 1:18–3:20, there is not much good news yet. This fact stimulated profitable discussions about why it's so important to understand the extent of the bad news before the good news will seem truly good.

5. **End with a review.** A review of a book is just like an overview—except it takes place at the end rather than the beginning. When you've completed examining all the book's pieces, take time to put them back together. You may even need to revise your overview in light of what you saw as you dug deeper through the details. So I find it helpful to dedicate an entire meeting to reviewing what we learned from the book, with respect to both themes and applications. This review may solidify the lessons and help people to remember them when they return to this book in future personal study.

Context, Context, Context

When you lead people in careful, contextual Bible study, you'll be amazed to see that some of your favorite memory verses don't actually mean what you once thought.

For example, when taken in context, Romans 8:28 doesn't mean that "all things" you could ever experience work together for whatever "good" you might dream of. No, Paul is saying specifically that all of "our present sufferings" (Romans 8:18–27) work together for that single good purpose which God predestined from the beginning: that we might be conformed to the image of his Son (Romans 8:29). So Romans 8:28 isn't a promise that everything will *feel* good and *seem* good to us. Rather, it's a promise that God will use everything for the very good purpose of making us more like Jesus. So it's less about comfort—in fact, it's more about the possibility of pain. But it's a pain that will make us more beautiful for having gone through it.

Keeping the context before your group at all times will go a long way toward preventing them from missing the author's main point.

Move the Group Toward the Main Point

The best piece of advice I received when I began blogging was to make sure each post had only one main point. I've not always followed the advice perfectly, but I've generally seen greater success when I do.

The same goes for Bible studies. Have you been part of a discussion that felt directionless? Have you tried to lead a discussion without being sure how to rein things in? You know you're there to study the

Bible, but how do you balance flexible compassion (giving people freedom to speak what's on their hearts) with intentional leadership?

The difference often lies simply in having a clear main point to work toward. How do you lead your group toward it?

The Main Point about the Main Point

One principle drives me: If (what I think is) the main point is truly the (biblical author's) main point, then I should be able to trace a path from any observation of the text to that main point. Therefore, I don't need my group to follow exactly the same path to the main point that my personal study followed. And I don't have to force the discussion into a certain rut, exhausting the group members and guaranteeing that I must remain the authoritative guru who has all the answers. People will never learn Bible study on their own that way.

An Example

In a meeting where my small group was studying Romans 2:1–16, my main point was that *God's wrath is revealed against moral, upright people who cannot practice what they preach*.

The main observations that led me to that main point were:

- Romans 2:1 contrasts with Romans 1:29–32.

Paul shifts from those who approve of evil behavior to those who disapprove of it.

- Repeated words, such as practice, righteous, condemn, does, law, and judge/judgment.
- Paul's use of Psalm 62 in Romans 2:6.

As we got into our discussion, however, group members observed very little of what I had observed. Other things in the text affected them:

- Romans 2:4 describes a lack of repentance as contempt for God's kindness.
- Repeated contrasts between Jews and Greeks in Romans 2:6–16.

One woman got especially hung up on Paul's claim in verse 11 that God shows no favoritism. "If God shows no favoritism," she remarked, "then why does Paul keep saying 'to the Jew first, and also to the Greek'!?" Others jumped in to assure her that Paul gives Jews first dibs on *both* reward and judgment, but she still struggled with the supposed claim to impartiality.

I could have tabled the discussion to get them back to the observations I thought most important. But the discussion was so juicy, and the members were forced to dive into the text to answer one another's questions. I didn't have the heart to cut that short.

But my key principle kicked in. If I was correct about the main point—that *God's wrath is revealed against moral, upright people who cannot practice what they preach*—I should be able to steer us in that direction, even from this discussion of God's impartiality. So with that perspective, I could celebrate the vigorous interactions and guide the group gently to the main idea by asking *why* Paul is so committed to clarifying God's impartiality. Our answer was that God's wrath plays no favorites! He's just as mad at the "good" people as he is at the "bad" people! All of them need the gift of his righteousness.

A Few Suggestions

In summary, the following suggestions will help you to lead your group toward the main point:

1. Come to the meeting prepared with a clear direction (a strong main point for the passage)

2. Hold your pathway to that main point loosely—let the discussion take on a life of its own

3. If the group sees things you haven't considered, be willing to reconsider what you thought was the main point

4. Keep asking "why?" questions until you help the group arrive at a clear main point

5. State the main point simply and clearly

6. Connect it to Jesus, and then move into application

People need your help to see the author's main point. But don't lead with such an iron fist that the discussion becomes an exercise in reading your mind. Lead in a way that inspires them with confidence to continue their study on their own. This will both motivate them to continue and build trust as you move them into application.

Encourage Heart-Oriented Application

Applying involves *believing*—this is the sphere of the head. John wrote his Gospel with one purpose: "so that you may believe that Jesus is the Christ, the Son of God" (John 20:31).

Yet applying also involves *doing*—this is about our hands. James wrote his epistle to highlight the "doing" life of the scattered people of God. "Be steadfast under trial," he said. "Be doers of the word." "Show no partiality." "Do not speak evil against one another." And so on. Theology is not absent from James, but it covers itself in thick layers of action and imperative.

Let us not forget, however, that applying is also about *loving and cherishing*—with the heart. We can know the truth and still be far from God (James 2:19). We can do all the right things and yet not come to the only one who can give us life (John 5:39–40).

As we lead Bible studies, we do well if we can help people to believe and do. But we must not neglect the opportunity we have, week in and week out, to help them deepen their love for God and be conformed to the image of his Son. Our application should target the heart above all.

How to Target the Heart in Bible Study Discussions

This is not rocket science, but it does require a little forethought and intention.

1. **Show them how to do it.** I've mentioned this before, but it's important enough to mention again. You must apply the Bible to your own heart, and you must do so publicly with your group. Only then will they see how it's done and that it's not so scary (Hebrews 13:7, Philippians 4:9, 1 Corinthians 11:1). Identify why vulnerability is hard for you, and repent.

2. **Ask about obstacles or hindrances.** When we hit a solid "do" application from the text, I find it helpful to ask people, "What keeps us from doing this thing God wants us to do?" When people answer that question honestly, they're usually cracking open the door to their hearts. The answer often reveals what they value more than obedience or more than the Lord himself.

3. **Suggest options.** Getting to the heart is not as complicated as some may think. We love something other than God, and good leaders

can expose those loves and show how Christ is better in every way. Are you concerned with what people think of you? What would happen if you didn't get that promotion, mobile device, spouse, or child you want?

4. **Celebrate progress.** We see more of what we reward, and in the process we foster micro-cultures. So when someone gets it and identifies character deficiencies or expresses desires for deep-seated change, I rejoice publicly. If I give more airtime to those folks than to those who want to discuss their third cousin's upcoming toenail surgery, the latter group learns quickly how to target their own hearts as well.

Praying in Bible Studies

Let me end this chapter with a brief note about prayer in Bible studies. Corporate prayer is a common practice for gatherings of believers, and that is right and good. But believe it or not, there is a time *not* to pray. In fact, there are many such times. Particularly if you want your Bible study to be inviting to non-Christians.

Imagine this: A coworker invites you to his house for dinner and a movie. Somewhere after the beef and potatoes, but before the surround sound explosions begin, he unrolls a few small mats. He says that before you can get to the evening's fun, you'll have to kneel with him and face toward Mecca to seek Allah's favor on your evening. The expectations are heavy, and he's not asking your opinion on the matter. How would you feel?

Let's not forget how others would feel if we expect them to take part in our religious rituals as well.

Now, I am not saying that there are more gods than one. Nor am I saying that all religions are equally valid. What I am saying is that love and respect should drive us to reconsider our customs so as not to set up unnecessary stumbling blocks.

By all means, let us pray without ceasing (1 Thessalonians 5:17). But that doesn't mean our prayers have to be audible. The Bible does not command us to begin or end every Bible study with corporate prayer.

Therefore, if your Bible study focuses on reaching non-Christians, I strongly suggest there be no praying out loud during the study. The gospel is already weird. Don't make your attempt to reach out any weirder than it needs to be.

Eleven

Life Outside the Meeting

Perhaps you've read this book to help you lead a meeting for a group of people studying God's Word. But I'm sure you know the work of God in these people's lives is not limited to the thirty to ninety minutes you spend discussing the Scripture together. In fact, that meeting time is primarily a time of planting. For the ministry of Christian discipleship to flourish, there must still be watering and patient waiting; otherwise the planted seed will not produce fruit. This chapter will address those "planting and waiting" leadership skills that spill outside the designated meeting time.

One Vital Behavior Determines the Success of Your Teaching Ministry

Have you participated in a Bible study led by someone lacking people skills? Have you attended Bible conferences where the celebrity speakers declined to hobnob with the proletariat? Have you taken a Bible class where everything you heard was true and precise, but you wondered if the professor had ever interacted with a live descendant of Adam?

Remember that the foundational mindset for preparing your Bible studies is one of dependence on the Lord (see Chapter 5). And fundamentally, that means you remain connected to the vine of Christ, the one who loved his friends by laying down his life for them. That mindset is not only for your *preparation*; it's also for your leadership, both during the Bible study meeting and outside it. If you stay connected to the vine, you will love as Christ has loved. And when you love as Christ has loved, your people will take notice and have an example to imitate.

> By this all people will know that you are my disciples, if you have love for one another. (John 13:35)

> Remember your leaders, those who spoke to you the word of God. Consider the outcome of their way of life, and imitate their faith. (Hebrews 13:7)

Therefore, to all who want to learn how to lead a Bible study, I commend one vital behavior above all others: *Love your people*. Get to know them. Learn their names and their histories. Find out what in life encourages them and what discourages them. Ask about their disappointments, dreams, and values. Make sure you understand them before you disagree with them. Find out why they come to the Bible study. Ask them regularly how they think it's going and how you can improve. Ask them what God is teaching them through it.

You'll never be able to do all these things during the meeting itself. Love requires investment; a price must be paid. You'll have to spend time with them (both in groups and one-on-one). You'll have to learn what they do for fun so you can learn to have fun doing it with them. You'll have to express your love in ways they feel loved, which won't necessarily be the same ways you like to express love. I write "you'll have to… you'll have to… you'll have to…" not because your righteousness depends on it, but because love has an inscrutable power of compulsion.

The Cost of Failure

The success of your Bible study—or of any teaching ministry—depends on this one vital behavior of loving your people. Is that a naïvely bombastic claim? I think not.

> If I speak in the tongues of men and of angels, but have not love, I am a noisy gong or a clanging cymbal. And if I have prophetic powers, and understand all mysteries and all knowledge, and if I have all faith, so as to remove mountains, but have not love, I am nothing. (1 Corinthians 13:1–2)

I've performed in orchestras when the gong and cymbals crashed at just the right time. Few earthly experiences are as moving as such powerful musical climaxes.

But I've also performed in orchestras when the

percussionist dropped the cymbals on the floor during the concert. Few earthly experiences are more embarrassing, more useless, or more counterproductive.

It is good for us to earnestly desire teaching gifts, and to be diligent to develop our teaching skills. But let us never forget: There is a still more excellent way (1 Corinthians 12:27–31).

The Reward of Love

I used to meet with a guy to study the Bible. He was a quick and humble learner, and he became a good friend. In general, our Bible study was not extraordinary, but profitable nevertheless. I remember, however, the day the Bible study shifted from being merely *profitable* to being *deeply rewarding*.

The girl of this young man's dreams had just broken up with him. He had the guts to meet with me anyway — were I in his place, I think I would have chosen to stay home in bed. Instead of having our regular discussion, I took him out and bought him the tallest mocha he could handle. Then we walked it off along a busy road and spoke of life, love, hurt feelings, and how God's Word had spoken to us in painful moments. Our time in the Word paid back many dividends that day and launched us into weeks of richer study than we had previously enjoyed together.

From the Lord's perspective, no Bible study will fully succeed unless the leader genuinely loves the participants (1 Corinthians 12:27–13:13). And one of the most tangible and effective ways to love people is simply to *get to know them*. In the case of that young man, I did something anyone would do, which was simply to listen, encourage, and enter his life. Most of the time, however, I'm too stingy to pay the cost of loving others. Love feels like an interruption. It requires more forethought or creativity than I'm willing to invest. And it takes me away from other, more "productive" tasks on my to-do list.

So when I struggle with the biblical call to invest in relationships (Mark 1:17, 1 Thessalonians 2:8, 2:17–3:13), I try to remember why it's worth it. That is, *why is it worth it to build relationships with people outside of the Bible study meeting?*

1. **It makes your application more relevant.** When you know what's going on in people's lives, you'll be more equipped to help them make specific application.

2. **It shows them Christ.** When people experience the personal care of their leader, it's easier for them to trust the personal care of the Lord Jesus.

3. **It sharpens your insight.** You'll know their highs and lows, and you'll be able to steer the Bible study discussion toward the very things they have on their minds.

4. **It bolsters your credibility.** When they know you care about them, they're more likely to

trust you. Then when you speak hard truths
from God's Word, that trust lubricates the
truth's pathway to their hearts.

Of course, we should love people because God wants
us to. And he made the world to work in such a way
that everyone benefits from honoring him. Therefore,
when you struggle to believe that love is worth the in-
convenience, remind yourself of how much more you
have to lose than a little time or forethought.

Community-Building Is Not Optional

As you engage in ministry, however, it doesn't take
long to realize the main thing working against you:
there's only one of you, but many of them. The hours
will run out long before you do all you could to love
and serve people, while remaining faithful to the other
responsibilities God has given you. You'll need help
to get the job done.

The fact that you need help to do ministry puts you
in good company. Even Jesus didn't do all the ministry
that could be done, by himself. He relied on the Holy
Spirit to carry on the work over the long term. We see
this especially in his upper room discourse, where he
spoke at length to his disciples of his coming departure
in order to save the world (John 13–16). He knew that
"his hour had come to depart out of this world" (John
13:1) and that he would no longer be physically present

to carry on his ministry. Yet he would not leave them as orphans; he would send help to be with them forever (John 14:16–19). It was to their advantage that he should depart and send this help (John 16:7–11).

So then, just as Jesus sent the Holy Spirit to help that particular community of disciples grow in love and faith, you can trust the Spirit's work to grow your people in love and faith. This means that you, as the leader, should not be the hub of ministry in the sense that everything good passes through you to the rest of the group. *You need the group members to help you love the group members.* Part of leadership is facilitating a God-honoring, Spirit-filled community where love, joy, peace, patience, kindness, goodness, faithfulness, gentleness, and self-control flow freely among the members. You can foster healthy relationships, attractive group dynamics, winsome recruiting, and redemptive counseling among group members.

If you fail at building community, the group may never outgrow your particular idiosyncrasies and insecurities as a leader. But if you succeed, the world just might realize you are his disciples (John 13:35), and you'll see mountains move.

Suggestions for Building Community

At the risk of sounding falsely humble, I must admit I don't have this community-building thing figured out. I have co-laborers in my church and in my ministry who are far better at fostering healthy community than I. But here are a few helpful ideas I've picked up over the years:

1. **Let love reach beyond the timeframe of the Bible study meeting.** If people think I care about them only during the ninety minutes of our meeting, they'll probably learn to limit their care for one another to the same time slot.

2. **Take initiative.** Ask people how they're doing. Remember what they tell you so you can ask them again later. If someone is disengaged from the group, ask a direct yet sensitive question to draw that person back in.

3. **Ask people to participate.** When people are good at something, find ways to ask them to do it for the group. Give them jobs, and they will gain a greater sense of ownership in the group.

4. **Have fun together.** If you don't have a sense of humor, buy one. People get exhausted when their conversation with you is only ever serious and personal. You'll seem more human when they can lower their defenses and simply have fun.

5. **Ask them to observe people.** If someone is struggling, ask others (without breaking confidences, of course) how they think that person is doing. Ask those people what they think would best serve the struggler.

6. **Give them real ministry responsibility.** Ask people to play a part in each other's lives. "Could you get lunch with Robert for a few weeks to encourage him through this difficult time?"

7. **Serve together.** Find tasks or service projects that need to be done in your church or community, and work on them together with your group. Nothing lowers defenses and grows relationships more than a little sweat and shared service, especially when you get outside of your normal routine together.

8. **Celebrate criticism.** My former pastor Tedd Tripp once showed me a remarkable attitude toward his critics. Instead of getting defensive, he chose to interpret criticism as the result of God's gifting on the critic. (That is, when you're gifted at something, you're likely to notice when others are less skilled in that area; therefore you'll be more inclined to offer criticism, hopefully of the constructive variety.) So he always thanks his critics and thanks God for them. Then whenever appropriate, he asks them to help fix the issue. Perhaps God put them there for that very purpose. This approach to criticism is fitting for leaders of all stripes. Don't become defensive or dismissive; choose to celebrate any and all criticism of you

or your leadership. And when appropriate, put the critics to work on the solution.

How to Measure Success

I want to believe that what I do matters, especially when I've put in much time and effort. Don't you?

The problem is, when we lead Bible studies, we are often tempted to measure success in the wrong ways. In fact, even using good criteria can sometimes be misleading. Consider these measures of success that were met in various situations of Scripture, but God was clearly not pleased with the overall result:

- "A lot of people come and the group is growing." This happens in Acts 19:29–41, but the result is confusion and persecution of God's people.

- "The meeting was exciting." In 1 Kings 18:28–29, the priests of Baal "raved on" all day, but it only ended up in their destruction.

- "I faithfully spoke the truth." Eliphaz speaks the truth to his friend Job in Job 5:8–16 (and the Apostle Paul even quotes that verse approvingly in 1 Corinthians 3:19). Yet Eliphaz spoke his truth at the wrong time and in the wrong circumstance (Job 42:7).

- "I followed all the steps and taught the right interpretation." One young lawyer understood the purpose of God's law precisely, yet he still found many excuses for not obeying it (Luke 10:25–28).

- "People feel close to each other." It is possible to unite a community around nefarious purposes (Genesis 11:1–9).

- "Defenses are being lowered." While vulnerability and transparency are to be commended, so are discernment and stalwart faith (Genesis 3:1–7).

- "People are learning so much." Just remember, it is possible to learn and learn and learn, and still never arrive at a knowledge of the truth (2 Timothy 3:6–7).

When I call these the "wrong ways" to measure success, I'm not suggesting any of them are inherently bad things. They become bad things only when divorced from the main thing.

The Main Measure of Success

What is the main thing? I addressed it in Chapter 1 when I explained the main reason to attend a Bible study. I now return to the same goal as a means to evaluate success: *As a result of the study, do people know God better through his Son Jesus Christ?*

If you remained faithful to the truth, there's a good chance you led them to the one who is the Truth. But if you didn't incarnate love in the process, you made a deafening noise without making an impact. That's not success.

If a lot of people came and felt comfortable with each other, but their affections and lives weren't conformed further to Christ's image, you may have merely accelerated someone's slide into hell.

If only a few people came, and you're consoling yourself that you're standing fast as one of the last faithful prophets in the land, it might be time to work on sweetening your speech and adding persuasiveness to your lips.

If people learned a lot, terrific. Did their increased knowledge increase their love for God and bolster their commitment to submit to Christ the Lord? Is it encouraging them to share the gospel of Jesus Christ with their families, neighbors, and coworkers?

The main measure of success is whether people know God any better through his Son Jesus Christ.

A personal, invasive evaluation like this can inspire fear in the stoutest leader's heart, as well it should—*Who am I to judge people's hearts?*—but let's not hesitate to speak clearly where God has spoken clearly. And God has spoken clearly about tests of genuine faith, or proofs that we have eternal life. We can use the principles within those tests to recognize the spiritual progress in others' lives, based on what they share with us. So God has provided means, therefore, by which you can evaluate whether your Bible study has been successful—that is, whether the people in it know God any better through his Son Jesus Christ.

Three Clear Tests

God gave us an entire book of the Bible to answer the question of what is true faith. That book can therefore teach you to recognize when you and others make *progress* in such faith. Consider this explicit purpose statement for John's first epistle:

> I write these things to *you who believe* in the name of the Son of God *that you may know that you have eternal life.* (1 John 5:13)

While John intended his Gospel to stimulate *faith* leading to eternal life (John 20:30–31), he intended his first letter to promote *assurance* of eternal life for those wondering whether their faith might be true faith.

John gives three clear and objective tests of genuine faith. [12] He states them early and returns to them repeatedly throughout.

1. **Keeping God's commandments**—the test of personal change

2. **Loving the brothers**—the test of personal affection

3. **Confessing Christ**—the test of personal witness

The first exposition of the tests of genuine faith occurs in 1 John 2 – but John repeats and develops the three tests repeatedly through the letter, climaxing with his closing statements. [13]

1. **Change** — "We know that everyone who has been born of God does not keep on sinning, but he who was born of God protects him, and the evil one does not touch him" (1 John 5:18). True faith makes progress in repenting of sin and resting in God's protection.

2. **Affection** — "We know that we are from God, and the whole world lies in the power of the evil one" (1 John 5:19). By this point in the letter, John has argued that to be "from God" is to love the brethren (see 1 John 4:7–12).

3. **Witness** — "And we know that the Son of God has come and has given us understanding, so that we may know him who is true; and we are in him who is true, in his Son Jesus Christ. He is the true God and eternal life. Little children, keep yourselves from idols." (1 John 5:20–21). True faith persists in confessing Jesus to be the Son of God who has come, the true God, and eternal life.

Applying the Tests

As you evaluate the success of your Bible study (or any other ministry), you'll want to observe attendance figures, participation levels, and the faithfulness of the leaders. But please don't neglect to ask the most important questions.

- As a result of the study, do people know God better through his Son Jesus Christ?
- How do we know?
    - *Are people changing to become more like Christ? Can we observe any area of their lives where they are making painful decisions to turn from sin and follow Jesus?*
    - *Do they have more affection for each other, and are they acting on it?*
    - *Are they persistently bearing witness to Jesus as the Son of God? Do they firmly believe it, and do they boldly declare it?*

John doesn't expect anyone to be perfect (1 John 1:8–10); neither should we. These questions aren't concerned with perfection, but with direction. Therefore, we can know that those who head in the right direction in all three areas have eternal life. We should return to these questions time and again as we evaluate the success of our Bible studies.

Twelve

The Best Way to Grow Your Bible Study Group

Why do you want to lead a Bible study? I trust you want to open the Scriptures to help others know God through his Son, Jesus Christ. Of course, our motives will always be mixed and imperfect until Christ returns. But may this desire to influence others toward Christ shine ever brighter.

As it does, you'll want to influence as many people as possible, right? That means you'll want your group to grow in both size and maturity. You won't be content if the group stays the same and never changes.

So this compels me to end this book with a critical question: *How do you grow the Bible study?*

I could answer this question in many practical ways, depending on your cultural background, environment, unique strengths and weaknesses, and the makeup of your current group. But this final chapter will highlight one fundamental growth technique you must master if you want to expand your reach for the Lord's sake.

> You then, my child, be strengthened by the grace
> that is in Christ Jesus, and what you have heard
> from me in the presence of many witnesses
> entrust to faithful men who will be able to teach
> others also. (2 Timothy 2:1–2)

Before you can master this technique, you must first *be strengthened by the grace that is in Christ Jesus* (2 Timothy 2:1). You will often feel unworthy for what you're about to do, and any time you feel worthy it will be even more urgent that you be strengthened by grace. Draw your sustenance and power from the lavish mercy and free forgiveness of your Master and King. You are approved to study the Bible (2 Timothy 2:15). And you are approved to lead others to study the Bible.

And what is this fundamental technique for growing your Bible study? "What you have heard from me in the presence of many witnesses entrust to faithful men who will be able to teach others also" (2 Timothy 2:2). *Take what you've learned and teach it to someone else.*

Pick someone with godly character in your group to be your assistant leader. Give that person some responsibility in the group. Follow a plan for progressively entrusting both the good deposit of the gospel and the skills of leadership. Your plan could look like this:[14]

1. **Come and see (John 1:39) — "I do, you watch."**
Invite this person to become your official
assistant leader. Meet with your assistant before
the group meeting to go over the passage.
Teach that person how to do OIA Bible study.
Practice it with that person over the course of a
few months.

2. **Come and follow me (Mark 1:17) — "I do, you
help."** Ask your assistant to evaluate your leadership and make suggestions for improvement.
Give your assistant particular assignments to
carry out during the meeting. "Please help me
to draw out the silent person." "Please feel free
to ask a key question if you think the discussion
is lagging." "Please come early and be ready to
help welcome people." "Please let me know
what you hear that will enable me to make the
next study more relevant to them."

3. **Go out and come back (Luke 10:1–24)
— "You do, I help."** Let your assistant lead one
of the meetings, and then meet to give that
person feedback on how it went. You now play
the support role during the meeting, helping
with difficult situations or participants. Be sure
to encourage your assistant with what went
well — and make sure you do that very soon
after the study has ended. In time, offer suggestions for improvement. Avoid correcting every

minor mistake; focus on broad patterns that might hold back this person's leadership ability.

4. **Go and make disciples (Matthew 28:18–20) — "You do, I watch."** Right when your assistant starts being truly effective, you'll need to send that person out to start a new group without you. This is painful, because it will feel like your own group is moving backwards. You'll lose the momentum and excitement of forward movement. But where there had been one group, now there are two. This is worth it.

After your assistant starts a new group, you'll probably want to continue meeting with him or her for a time. You'll want to discuss how their group goes as it gets off the ground. You'll discuss the new challenges and opportunities faced by this fledgling leader. But most of all, you'll want to make sure the new leader wastes no time in looking for a new assistant to train. And you'll be looking for another assistant yourself. And before you know it, you'll have four groups going.

I didn't invent this model for growth. Jesus instituted it from the start of his ministry, and it has been changing the world ever since. It's not flashy, and you'll rarely be able to wow people with your dramatic growth figures. ("I trained one new person this year!") But the power of multiplication is like an encrypted virus, wreaking havoc on the forces of darkness. Don't neglect this best way to grow your Bible study group.

Before you know it, the seed you planted will "bear fruit, thirtyfold and sixtyfold and a hundredfold" (Mark 4:20).

There's a surprising glory in leading a group of ordinary people to open their Bibles, read what's on the page, and discuss how God might use those words to change the world.

APPENDIX: SAMPLE BIBLE STUDY LEADER'S NOTES

Exodus 12:29–13:16

Launching question: *What is the most important thing you would like to be remembered for in the future?*

Main Point: Future generations must know that Yahweh owns firstborn (=everything) and remakes his creation at will.

Supporting Truths:
- This very day is special (12:29, 41, 51, 13:3, 4, 8, 10)
- This occasion must be celebrated (12:43, 47, 13:3, 5, 8, 14)
- God owns all the firstborn—a picture of everyone and everything

Outline:

12:29–42 —Thorough victory against Egypt; departure in haste

12:43–51 — Ordinance of the Passover: God determines who, when, and how to eat (future-oriented?)

13:1–2 — God owns every firstborn (ownership of the future)

13:3–16 — Remember this day
- No yeast for 7 days (13:3–10)
  —when YHWH brings you in, tell your sons how God brought you out so his law would be in your mouth
- Redeem all the firstborn (13:11–16)
  —when YHWH brings you in, tell your sons of God's mighty hand that killed Egyptian firstborn but brought us out

Connection to Christ: Jesus is the firstborn of all creation. Through his death and resurrection, we've been brought out of one kingdom and into another. We are no longer strangers and enemies but spotless, unblemished, living sacrifices. See Col 1:13–23.

Observation/Interpretation Questions to help lead to the main point:

1. What happened that Passover night?

2. How are they to remember that night?

3. Why are they to remember that night?

Applications:

For ourselves:

- What difference does it make that God owns you? That he redeemed you by killing his firstborn son?
- What must you do now to prepare future generations for this message of redemption?
  - act as parent/prepare to become a parent
  - invest in the future of the church

For our Growth Group:

- How can we make sure our Growth Group can remember these things?
- How can we welcome foreigners and strangers and become more effective at leading people to know Christ's redemption?

For our church:

- What must we do to prepare future generations of leaders and members?

For the world:

- How does the world view ownership? Who owns me?
- How does the world view the future or the good of mankind?

AUTHOR

Peter Krol has taught the Bible since 1996 both as a collegiate missionary with DiscipleMakers (www.dm.org) and as an elder in both Presbyterian and Independent churches. He's trained dozens of people to study the Bible. Many of them now train others who, in turn, have begun training a third generation. With each new year, he reads nothing but the Bible until he finishes the Bible—not because it makes God any happier with him, but because it makes him happier with God in Christ.

ACKNOWLEDGMENTS

This book is the product of more than twenty years serving in campus ministry with DiscipleMakers (**www.dm.org**). I'm not sure how to capture and appropriately acknowledge the contributions of all who have had a hand in training me to lead small group Bible studies, shaping my thinking about small groups, or inspiring my vision for teaching God's Word through interactive discussion groups. But this book is a monument to the profound effectiveness of this ministry and the extraordinary giftedness and commitment of both current and former staff members. May this book help others to see the surprising glory you have basked in for decades, the glory of simply leading groups of ordinary people to open their Bibles, read what's on the page, and discuss how God might use those words to change the world. It's been my privilege to partner with such amazing fellow workers for the truth.

I'm grateful for the members of my executive leadership team—Beth Dripps, Ben Hagerup, and Tom Hallman—who rallied together to cover the bases and allow me a few months of focused writing time to complete the manuscript. Thank you for your enthusiasm for this resource!

Ryan Higginbottom is not only an exceptional professor of mathematics, but also a sharp Bible study leader—and an even sharper coach of Bible study leaders. Thanks for your contribution to my own thinking and to the material in this book. I praise God for you, the rare sort of friend who endures at sticking closer than a brother.

Thanks are due to Dan Miller and Caleb Olshefsky for the graphics within this book, and especially to Caleb for the invaluable concept work on the cover design.

This book would also be far less enjoyable to read, and have far more gaps in its argumentation, were it not for the magic arts of my word-wizard wife, Erin, and my editors Dave Swavely and Kevin Meath. Thank you for your delightful and fruitful partnership.

ENDNOTES

1. A version of this abridgment also appeared in the appendix of *Can I Smoke Pot?* by Tom Breeden and Mark L. Ward, Jr. (Cruciform Press, 2016).

2. See my collection of blog posts at https://www.knowableword.com/tag/structure/ for further instruction on how and why to grasp the structure of a passage.

3. This model for preparing and leading a Bible study is heavily influenced by Colin Marshall's terrific book, *Growth Groups,* Matthias Media, 1995.

4. For further reflection on both our reasons and the Bible's cure for invulnerability, see the groundbreaking work, Joseph W. Smith III, *Transparency: A Cure for Hypocrisy in the Modern Church* (CreateSpace, 2018).

5. You're free to disagree, of course, but I conclude that, in this paragraph, Paul's lone imperative expresses the main thing he wishes to communicate to Timothy. Yet even if you disagree with respect to Paul's main point, I trust your disagreement won't distract from *my* main point in this illustration: that your presentation of the same main point from the same passage can take a very different shape for different audiences.

6. Matthias Media, 1995, p. 39.

7. Ibid.

8. This introduction and the following sections on Six Characteristics, Observation, Interpretation, and Application were first written for the Knowable Word blog (www.knowableword.com) by my fellow contributor Ryan Higginbottom. They are reprinted here with slight editing, and with permission.

9. See Chapter 2 for more detail on the method itself.

10. Find some good advice for such situations at https://www.smallgroups.com/articles/2012/help-my-small-group-has-been-hijacked.html and https://www.ocfusa.org/2009/09/small-group-detours/.

11. Quotes found in the *New York Times* between November 9 and November 15, 2014.

12. Please understand that I am not suggesting that these three tests enable you to *determine* who has eternal life. There is only one Judge who can do that. These tests simply enable you to *recognize* ("that you may know...") those moving in the direction of eternal life. Thus, the teaching of 1 John offers both guidance for self-evaluation (e.g. 1 John 2:1-17) and the discernment to resist being deceived by either the false profession or false teaching of others (1 John 1:6, 8, 10; 2:18-19, 22, 26; 3:7-10; 4:1-3, 20; 5:10-12). The letter's tagline is "We know," implying that *these are not secret things belonging to God but have been revealed by him so we may observe them.* John Stott's commentary on *The Epistles of John* (Eerdmans, 1964) provides a helpful analysis of 1 John, explaining the three tests in great detail.

13. We see these three themes in 1 John 2: change (1 John 2:3-6), affection (1 John 2:7-11), witness (1 John 2:18-25).

14. I first heard the following four categories and their labels from a former colleague, David Kieffer. He claims not to have invented it, but to have heard it from his former pastor Drew Derreth. Pastor Derreth claims to have heard it from someone else. Unfortunately, I cannot cite a root source for this rubric, but I must still disclose the fact that it's not original to me.

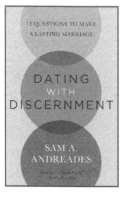

Dating with Discernment:
12 Questions to Make a
Lasting Marriage

Sam A. Andreades | 280 pages

A fresh, biblical paradigm for choosing a spouse.

"This is a brilliant book!" – Rosaria Butterfield
"Profoundly insightful" – Joel R. Beeke

bit.ly/DatingWell

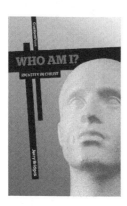

Who Am I?
Identity in Christ

Jerry Bridges | 91 pages

*Jerry Bridges unpacks Scripture to give the
Christian eight clear, simple, interlocking answers
to one of the most essential questions of life.*

bit.ly/WHOAMI

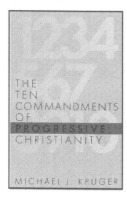

The Ten Commandments of
Progressive Christianity

Michael J. Kruger | 56 pages

*A cautionary look at ten dangerously appealing
half-truths.*

bit.ly/TENCOM

Endorsed by Collin Hansen,
Kevin DeYoung, Michael Horton

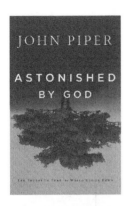

Astonished by God
Ten Truths to Turn the World Upside Down

John Piper | 192 pages

Turn your world on its head.

bit.ly/AstonishedbyGod

The Joy Project:
An Introduction to Calvinism

(with Study Guide)

Tony Reinke
Foreword by John Piper | 168 pages

True happiness isn't found. It finds you.

bit.ly/JOYPROJECT

Preparing for Marriage
Help for Christian Couples

John Piper | 86 pages

As you prepare for marriage, dare to dream with God.

bit.ly/prep-for-marriage

Don't miss these fully inductive Bible studies for women from Keri Folmar!

Loved by churches. Endorsed by Kristi Anyabwile, Connie Dever, Gloria Furman, Kathleen Nielson, and Diane Schreiner.

The series currently consists of six volumes.

10 weeks   *10 weeks*   *10 weeks*

Joy! (Philippians)   *Faith* (James)   *Grace* (Ephesians)

11 weeks   *11 weeks*   *9 weeks*

Son of God (Gospel of Mark, 2 volumes)   *Zeal* (Titus)

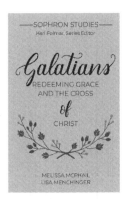

Galatians: Redeeming Grace and the Cross of Christ

Melissa McPhail and Lisa Menchinger
184 pages

Introducing the Sophron Series, a new Bible study series for women. Keri Folmar, Series Editor.

bit.ly/Sophron-Galatians

•

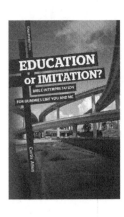

Education or Imitation?
Bible Interpretation for Dummies Like You and Me

Curtis Allen | 87 pages

How can we interpret Scripture rightly? Imitate Jesus.

bit.ly/IMITATE

The Company We Keep
In Search of Biblical Friendship

Jonathan Holmes
Foreword by Ed Welch | 112 pages

Biblical friendship is deep, honest, pure, tranparent, and liberating. It is also attainable.

bit.ly/B-Friend

Devoted
Great Men and Their Godly Moms

Tim Challies | 128 pages

Women shaped the men who changed the world.

bit.ly/devotedbook

Run to Win:
The Lifelong Pursuits of a Godly Man

Tim Challies | 163 pages

Plan to run, train to run…run to win.

bit.ly/RUN2WIN

Do More Better
A Practical Guide to Productivity

Tim Challies | 114 pages

Don't try to do it all. Do more good. Better.

bit.ly/domorebetter

Made in the USA
Columbia, SC
28 July 2022

64215949R00098